The 20 British Prime Ministers
of the 20th century

Callaghan

HARRY CONROY

HAUS PUBLISHING • LONDON

First published in Great Britain in 2006 by
Haus Publishing Limited
26 Cadogan Court
Draycott Avenue
London SW3 3BX

www.hauspublishing.co.uk

A CIP catalogue record for this book is available from the British Library

ISBN 1-904950-70-1

Designed by BrillDesign
Typeset in Garamond 3 by MacGuru Ltd
info@macguru.org.uk

Printed and bound by Graphicom, Vicenza

Front cover: John Holder

Contents

Part One

THE LIFE

Chapter 1: Early Life

If any politician had cause to agree with Harold Macmillan's reply when asked what shaped the course of his political career ('events, dear boy, events'), it was Leonard James Callaghan. Events dictated Callaghan's life from the moment his father died when he was aged only nine, through to the 'Wind of Change' which was beginning to sweep through Britain's African colonies when he was Shadow Colonial Secretary, to the Six Day War in the Middle East when he was Chancellor of the Exchequer. There then followed the outbreak of 'The Troubles' in Northern Ireland in 1969 during his time as Home Secretary. Finally the 1978–9 'Winter of Discontent' when he was Prime Minister, accompanied by the referendum on devolution in Scotland, which lead to his defeat in the 1979 general election at the hands of Margaret Thatcher. All these events shaped Jim Callaghan's political career. Few dreamt that the son born to James and Charlotte Callaghan in very modest circumstances in Portsmouth on 27 March 1912 would rise to the pinnacle of political power in Britain, as the country's Prime Minister.

The Callaghans already had a daughter Dorothy, who had been born in 1904, when their baby son arrived. His father, the son of an Irish Catholic immigrant who had fled to England following the potato famine in Ireland, had run away from home to join the Royal Navy in the 1890s. He was a year too young to enlist so gave a false date of birth and changed his surname from Garogher to Callaghan so that his parents could not be traced and his subterfuge uncovered. A Roman Catholic by birth, Callaghan Senior fell in love with Charlotte, a Baptist and already a widow, her first husband having died in a naval accident in Plymouth Sound. Marriage to members of another denomination, however, were forbidden in the Catholic Church at that time, and a Royal Navy Catholic Chaplain refused to marry the couple. James Callaghan Snr vowed to have nothing more to do with the Church he had been born into and married Charlotte in a Baptist chapel.

The elder James Callaghan enjoyed an adventurous career in the Royal Navy. He rose to the rank of Chief Petty Officer and took part in an armed expedition to Benin City in Nigeria which ended in the city being destroyed by fire. This sense of adventure led him applying to join Scott's expedition to the Antarctic on HMS *Discovery* but his wife, having already lost one husband in her young life, dissuaded him from this idea. Instead he joined the crew of the Royal Yacht which was based at Portsmouth. This posting gave the Callaghans a brief experience of a normal family life. King Edward VII and Queen Alexandra were only infrequent users of the yacht and while in port the crew would report for duty in the morning and like any employee in Civvy Street would return to their homes in the evening.

However their son, baptised Leonard James Callaghan, was too young to have any recollection of this period, and when the First World War broke out James Callaghan Snr joined the battleship HMS *Agincourt* at Scapa Flow. The result was that Jim Callaghan's first memory of his father had to wait until his father was demobbed in 1919 when the younger Callaghan was seven years old. Charlotte Callaghan, like the thousands of other servicemen's wives, was left to bring up their two children on her own while her husband was at war. The family spent the war years in their terraced family home in Copnor, a working class area to the north of Portsmouth. Mrs Callaghan was a devout Baptist and her children attended Sunday School. Indeed in his autobiography *Time and Chance* James Callaghan recalls that most of Sunday was spent at church with Sunday Schools in the morning and afternoon in addition to a church service. The young Callaghan in his early years was known as Leonard until he entered politics in 1945 when he decided to be known by his middle name James and thereafter became known as Jim or James. To avoid confusion for the purposes of this book I have used Jim throughout.

Following his demob Callaghan Senior joined the Coast-guard which meant the family moving to the fishing village of Brixham at Torbay, Devon. A cottage went with the job and the young Jim Callaghan began the happiest years of his childhood, but sadly they were to be short-lived, for, after only two years, his father died at the age of 44. However, in this short period a close bond quickly developed between father and son. The memories of these years remained with him throughout his life. The family's cottage stood close to a pebble beach, while his father carried out his duties from a cabin perched at the top of Berry Head overlooking the entrance to Torbay. His duties entailed keeping a look-out for ships in distress and also contacting other coastguard stations dotted along the English Channel by Morse giving details of ship movements. The youthful Callaghan would often accompany his father to his cliff-top cabin where he was introduced to the mysteries of Morse Code and signal flags. The pair would search for gull eggs when the weather allowed, and when stormy conditions confined them to the cabin the former Chief Petty Officer would regale his son with his adventures at sea. The bond of trust between father and son was so strong that when Callaghan Snr was called out to rescue the crew of a ship which had run aground in a storm-lashed Torbay he took his son with him. Callaghan Jnr helped to winch the crew to safety from their stricken ship. This purple period in young Callaghan's childhood came to an end in the autumn of 1921 when his father became ill and was admitted to the Naval Hospital at Plymouth where he died. Jim Callaghan later wrote: *Thus ended the shortest and happiest period of my childhood.*

By contrast the period following his father's death was to be the most difficult of his life. The family was plunged into poverty. They were allowed to live in the Coastguard cottage for a short time then had to rely on the charity of a member of the Brixham Baptist Chapel who gave shelter to the hapless family. Charlotte Callaghan had no income and Jim would gather scraps of wood from the local shipyard for fuel. He would also visit the local fishmarket twice a week where a member of the Baptist Chapel would give him scraps of fish. Then in 1923 Charlotte Callaghan returned with her family to Portsmouth where they were constantly on the move between different rented rooms. It was during this time that the young Callaghan received his first taste of politics. One of the family's many landladies was a Mrs Long, a Scot. She was a member of the Labour Party and during the general elections of 1923 and 1924 she would send the schoolboy with messages to Labour Party committee rooms.

The family's financial circumstances were improved when in 1924, following the election of the first Labour government, Mrs Callaghan was granted a pension on the basis that her husband's death was partly due to his war service. The Ministry of Pensions also agreed to pay Jim Callaghan's school fees of two guineas a term when he passed the entrance exams.

However, this was an unhappy chapter in Jim Callaghan's life. No doubt still trying to overcome the loss of his father, he did not apply himself to his schoolwork and had to be reproached by his mother who was only too aware that the Ministry of Pensions paid his school fees on the understanding that his exam results showed that he was applying himself. Thankfully the penny dropped for Callaghan before the axe fell and he began to put more effort into his studies, which led to him gaining the Senior Oxford Certificate. This qualified him for entry into a university but in common with generations of working class families, paid work was the first priority after completing full-time education and in 1929 Jim Callaghan sat the Civil Service Entrance Exam. There is no doubt that Callaghan regretted that he was not encouraged to aim for university, remarking in his biography of his mother's desire that he should gain employment with a pension at the end – *It was not much of an ambition to hold out to a boy, but I suppose she was influenced by her own past insecurity.*[1] Many children of working class families have shared Callaghan's disappointment and this experience was to influence both his attitude and decisions in his later working life as a trade union official and politician.

At the age of 17 Jim Callaghan struck out on his own. He passed the Civil Service Entrance Exam and was appointed to a junior position in the Inland Revenue Tax Office at Maidstone in Kent at a salary of £52 a year plus a cost of living allowance of 15 shillings a week (75p). Once again the Baptist Church came to the aid of the Callaghan family, helping to find him lodgings in Maidstone. Despite his disappointment at not advancing to university Callaghan had a great deal to be thankful for as in November 1929 'Black Thursday' marked the Wall Street crash in the United States and the onset of mass unemployment in Britain.

It was in the unlikely setting of rural Maidstone, in the stuffy environment of the Inland Revenue, that Jim Callaghan embarked on the journey which was to culminate in his becoming Prime Minister 47 years later. He joined the Maidstone Labour Party and the Association of the Officers of Taxes (AOT) which represented the clerical grades within the Inland Revenue. It was also at this time while teaching Sunday School at the local Baptist Chapel that he met Audrey Moulton, a 16-year-old who was still a pupil at the local grammar school. It was the start of a life-long love affair.

In modern times Jim Callaghan would have been described as a 'Young Turk'. Having discovered socialism and trade unionism he was a young man in a hurry. Within a year of joining he had become office secretary of the union. In common with many young activists in every generation of the 20th century he had little time for the national executive of the union and wrote critical articles in the union journal. His youthful arrogance came to the fore when he suggested to the hierarchy of the Inland Revenue that the AOT did not represent new entrants such as himself. He had still to learn that unity is strength.

However, his trade union and political activities did not hinder his studies for promotion and in 1932 he passed the Civil Service examination which allowed him to become a senior tax officer. The same year he was elected Kent branch secretary of the AOT. The following year he attended his first union conference in Buxton and was elected to the union's national executive council. This did not deter him agitating within the union for better conditions and more opportunities for new entrants to the Inland Revenue. A 'New Entrants Movement' was formed within the AOT, led by Callaghan and Stanley Raymond who in later years was Chairman of British Railways and whom Callaghan when he was Home Secretary appointed Chairman of the Gaming Board in 1968.

The 'New Entrants Movement' campaigned vigorously against the rigid structure of the Inland Revenue which restricted those who joined the Service from school to lower clerical grades with little prospect of promotion to higher administration strata which was the exclusive province of university graduates. Perhaps this was an early indication of Jim Callaghan's resentment that those such as himself who had not had the opportunity to go on to university through the financial circumstances of their families should have a glass ceiling imposed on their careers. The 'New Entrant Movement' was short-lived, like many other similar internal trade union agitation organisations. It was wound up in June 1934 but it drew the attention of the AOT's leadership, headed by General Secretary Douglas Houghton, to their legitimate grievance and the union began to tackle the issue.

In 1934 the Inland Revenue Service transferred Jim Callaghan to London. Audrey followed him and became a domestic science teacher. She was also interested in politics and joined the Fabians. Along with Jim she attended lectures given by Harold Laski. Audrey also attended economic lectures given by the future Labour leader Hugh Gaitskell. The move to London led Callaghan to become a protégé of Douglas Houghton. Callaghan credits the influence of Houghton for his being appointed by the NEC in August 1936 to the full-time post of Assistant Secretary of the AOT. This was the same year in which the AOT merged with the National Association of Tax Assessing and Collection Services (NATACS) to form the Inland Revenue Staff Federation (IRSF). The union was further enlarged when a year later the Valuation Officers' Clerical Association joined. Callaghan and Houghton's careers crossed on many occasions with Houghton becoming

Labour MP for Sowerby in 1949, rising to serve as a minister in Harold Wilson's first government.

Callaghan and Audrey married on Audrey's birthday, 28 July 1938, in Knightrider Baptist Church in Maidstone. Although extremely happy in their personal lives they lived under the shadow of the gathering war clouds in Europe with the German *Luftwaffe* honing their terror attacks in the Spanish Civil War. Both Callaghan and Audrey, who had joined the Labour Party in 1931, campaigned for the British government to lift the arms embargo against the Republicans as they were the legitimate government of Spain. Callaghan also managed to persuade the IRSF to send financial aid to the Spanish Medical Aid Committee.

Shortly after their marriage the danger of war heightened when Germany occupied Czechoslovakia. When war was finally declared in September 1939 Audrey was expecting their first child, Margaret. Soon after hostilities began Callaghan's inherent political beliefs were revealed when he committed to paper how he wanted the United Kingdom to emerge at the end of the conflict. The 27-year-old trade unionist was already looking towards the end of the British Empire, suggesting that our colonies be transferred to an International Commission and Britain to give up its preferential trade terms in our 'overseas possessions'. He also wanted India to be given genuine Home Rule. At home his ambition was for the British government to support a policy of full employment and major industries such as coal, textiles and agriculture to be subject to a national plan. After the defeat of Nazism he argued against further new small European states being created as this would result in political tension but called for the removal of economic barriers to encourage free trade. Little was the middle-ranking trade union official to realise that he was to carry these far-sighted concepts with him into Parliament following the end of the Second World War and that they would remain with him as he rose through the parliamentary ranks to become Prime Minister, allowing him to exert influence on how Britain shed its colonial possessions and developed relationships with the rest of Europe. He was also to remain loyal to the belief in full employment.

The outbreak of the Second World War was to herald a period of radical change in the Callaghan household. Eventually the war saw him follow his father into the Royal Navy and also his transformation from a trade union official into a budding politician. At the start of hostilities with London facing bombardment by the Luftwaffe the IRSF followed the Inland Revenue when it moved out of Somerset House in the Capital to Llandudno in Wales where it established its wartime headquarters. Callaghan was delegated to find office accommodation for the union in the Welsh seaside town, and secured premises in an empty boarding house. This led to the Callaghan's also leaving their London home with Audrey moved into the flat above the new premises with their newborn daughter Margaret. Callaghan divided his time between Llandudno and London sleeping in the basement of his office in St George's Square when in the Capital. The family remained in Wales until near the end of 1944.

Following the evacuation of the British Expeditionary Force from Dunkirk in May 1940 Callaghan volunteered to join the Royal Navy as a seaman but Houghton intervened, insisting that Callaghan could not be spared. Trade union officials were deemed to be in a 'reserved occupation' and this put an end to Callaghan's first attempt to go to war. His willingness to serve in the armed forces did not mean that Callaghan was willing to give unquestioning support to policies just because they were described as part of the war effort, however. He was among the 1,000 trade union officials who attended a meeting addressed by Minister of Labour Ernest Bevin in the Central Hall, Westminster on 25 May 1940 during which Bevin called on the trade unions to sacrifice some of their hard-won rights to aid the war effort. Callaghan set out his reply in an article in the union journal which, while giving broad support to Bevin's call for co-operation, attacked the proposed wage stabilisation measures while large hotels were full of guests who did not appear to be sharing the economic burden others were expected to bear. He also advocated more price controls and some upward adjustment of wages.

Callaghan continued to display his radical tendencies when he argued that in return for the sacrifices made during the war the working class should benefit financially in the post-war period. He disagreed with Sir Stafford Cripps, whom he met on Cripps' return from a spell as the United Kingdom's ambassador in Moscow, that there should be a 'National Government' after the war. Callaghan's interest in wider politics had led him to become a prospective Labour candidate. The IRSF, although barred from controlling its political fund under the terms of the 1927 Trades Dispute Act, had managed to find a loophole by placing £1,500 in the hands of independent trustees to be used to help his election campaign.

Shortly after Callaghan's second daughter Julia was born in October 1942 Houghton finally agreed that Callaghan could join the Royal Navy because in Cyril Plant he had found a replacement for him as Assistant Secretary. In his *Time and Chance* Callaghan admitted that he had second thoughts about leaving behind his wife and two young daughters to go off to war but having made such a nuisance of himself felt he could not back out!

He mistakenly believed that the Royal Navy Patrol Service included the motor torpedo boats and applied to join it. His application was successful and he was instructed to report for duty to Lowestoft only discover that he had got it wrong and that rather than bouncing along on top of the waves he would be serving on a rather slower minesweeper. His training took him to Lamlash on the Isle of Arran in the Firth of Clyde where he was put forward for promotion to sub-lieutenant. While training for the promotion he had to go through a medical examination which revealed that he had tuberculosis, resulting in him being admitted to Haslar Hospital near Portsmouth. Following a spell in hospital he was discharged but was informed he would be confined to shore duties for six months with the Admiralty in Whitehall where his promotion to sub-lieutenant was confirmed and he was given the task of writing a manual on Japan, a country he knew nothing about. Once he had completed the manual, *The Enemy Japan*, Callaghan was impatient to get to sea and was horrified when he was told that now he was an expert on Japan the plan was to send him to Australia to join the British Pacific Fleet. Callaghan successfully protested and he sailed on HMS *Activity*, a former merchant vessel, to join the East Indies Fleet in Ceylon.

Callaghan was encouraged to put his name forward for the Cardiff South seat by Dai Kneath, a member of the IRSF National Executive from Swansea who, while Callaghan was on leave, took him to meet Bill Headon, the local secretary of the Labour Party. His surname led Mr Headon's wife to suspect that the young naval officer might be a Roman Catholic and she asked him outright. Having been assured that he was in fact a Baptist the good lady explained that if he had been a Catholic she would have supported another candidate who was a Methodist! One of the shortlist of three turned out to be George Thomas, Callaghan scraped through by 12 votes to 11 over Thomas. It was 1943, and Callaghan, who had attended the selection conference in his naval uniform immediately, rejoined his ship and did not return to Cardiff until the general election was called two years later.

He admitted that he did not have a particularly exciting war or for that matter particularly dangerous. However, it gave him experience of Britain's Senior Service which was to serve him well in his political career giving him an insight into the far flung-British Empire which he put to go use as shadow colonial spokesman and later Foreign Secretary.

On VE Day, 8 May 1945 Callaghan was serving on HMS *Queen Elizabeth* in the Indian Ocean. Following the victory in Europe the coalition government was dismantled and preparations began for a general election. Along with other prospective candidates serving in the forces Callaghan was allowed to return home. The young Callaghan knew that he was returning home to fight a winnable seat. The sitting Conservative member, Sir Arthur Evans, was first elected in 1923, losing the seat to Labour in 1929 before regaining it in 1931. In the last general election before the formation of a coalition government following the outbreak of the War, he scraped through with a 541 majority over Labour. The constituency has several working class areas

The Beveridge Report was drawn up by the economist Sir William Beveridge. The report aimed to eradicate the humiliation of the means testing carried out in the 1930s before the unemployed or sick received help. It proposed a free health service, unemployment benefit and also a death grant to pay funeral expenses creating the concept of the state caring for its citizens from cradle to grave. The report heralded the Welfare State which saw the creation of the National Health Service in 1946. The reforms were to be paid by the introduction of the National Insurance scheme.

including Adamsdown, the old Irish quarter as well as the dockland areas of Tiger Bay and Bute Town although these were balanced by middle class areas such as Penarth.

The Beveridge Report on Social Insurance had been published in December 1942 and Labour's manifesto *Let Us Face the Future* supported the radical proposals contained in the Beveridge Report and demanded the nationalisation of major industries such as coal and steel as well as a policy of full employment. Many voters recalled the mass unemployment of the 1930s and did not trust the Conservatives to provide full employment.

Labour won a landslide victory on 26 July, winning 393 seats compared to the Conservatives' 213. Callaghan won Cardiff South with a stunning 6,000 majority over the Conservative candidate Evans. He attracted 17,489 votes to Evans' 11,545. He had campaigned on the rapid demobilisation of the armed forces, a new house-building programme, price and rent control and for the creation of an international armed force responsible to a World Authority. So the year that his son Michael was born, Callaghan became one of more than 250 Labour MPs elected who were new to Parliament. They were members of the most radical government Britain has ever known.

Chapter 2: The Attlee Government

There can be few periods in British history which can compare with what faced the Labour government of 1945. The country had just emerged from a world war, millions of servicemen were looking forward to being demobilised and the public believed they had earned the right to expect a better Britain than they had left behind. The British public voted in a Labour government committed to a programme designed to bring full employment while at the same time introducing the reforms proposed in the Beveridge Report giving individuals financial protection against sickness and unemployment. At the same time a National Health Service free at the point of use was established. Labour's Prime Minister, Clement Attlee, had also pledged to bring major industries such as steel and mining into public ownership, measures welcomed by the employees of these industries who believed that government ownership would be more enlightened than that of the existing private owners.

Few realised the full extent to which the war had impoverished the country. The Lend-Lease arrangement with the USA government had helped finance Britain's war effort but it came as a shock when the American government abruptly ended this arrangement within three weeks of the new Parliament's first session. With no time to catch its breath, the war-ravaged country was suddenly faced with a financial crisis brought about by its wartime ally demanding its pound of flesh. There was certainly no whiff of the special relationship about the US action and Jim Callaghan was a vocal critic of the USA when the full import of the decision was finally realised as Britain was forced to negotiate a massive $3.75 billion loan from America to literally keep the country afloat.

Francis Beckett in his biography of Attlee quotes the Labour Prime Minister, speaking several years later, as absolving President Harry Truman of deliberately acting to damage Britain's interests saying: 'I doubt if the American administration realised how serious the blow which they struck. Truman ... had become President on the death of Franklin Roosevelt after less than three months as Vice President. He had no experience of international affairs and Roosevelt had not kept him in touch with them. He signed the paper put in front of him without thinking about its implications.'[1]

This generous interpretation of Truman's actions was not shared by Callaghan at the time, and certainly the tough terms which the Americans imposed does not point to the American administration feeling that they owed Britain any favours. The entire episode points rather to the USA being motivated towards establishing themselves as a world power at the expense of Britain who became the junior partner in any relationship.

The economist Lord Keynes was despatched by Attlee to negotiate a loan which he did but only after having to accept rigorous conditions. The loan was debated in the House of Commons on 13 December 1945. The British government was required to pay a commercial interest rate of 2 per cent in 50 annual instalments and agree to two far-reaching conditions. Britain had to accept the immediate multilateral liberalisation of trade and the convertibility of Sterling into dollars to come into effect in July 1947. There was opposition within the Cabinet to the terms of the loan but the harsh economic reality was that the government had little choice. Jim Callaghan did not speak during the often-heated debate in the Commons but voted along with other Labour MPs such as Michael Foot and Barbara Castle against accepting the loan on such terms. There were 23 Labour rebels, plus more than 70 Conservative MPs, who voted against accepting the loan. Callaghan had earlier been appointed Parliamentary Private Secretary to John Parker, Parliamentary Under-Secretary at the Dominions Office, a position he resigned from following the vote. It is difficult to exaggerate the financial crisis which resulted in the ending of Lend-Lease and the impact of the terms of the subsequent loan. It has been argued that the effects were still being felt when the UK was forced to devalue in 1968 when Callaghan was Chancellor of Exchequer.

The newly-elected MP, however, was learning his trade as a politician as these great events of state unfolded. His experience in the Royal Navy during the war had whetted his interest in foreign affairs and in December 1945 he joined a parliamentary delegation on a visit to Russia alongside the Scottish miners' leader Lawrence Daly. The delegation visited Moscow, Stalingrad and Kiev. During their visit to Kiev Callaghan attended the trial of a German officer accused of murdering Jewish children. The major rift between the Allies had yet to happen. Callaghan was among the many, particularly in the Labour Party, who did not foresee the breakdown of international relationships leading to tanks of the former Allies facing each other across the border between East and West Germany. The irony that a war which had been declared ostensibly to protect the security of smaller countries such as Poland ended with the Soviet army occupying Poland and a host of other European countries including Hungary and Romania. In March 1946 while visiting the US, Winston

Churchill introduced the term 'Iron Curtain' into the English language, Callaghan was among the 92 Labour MPs who signed a motion denouncing the speech as endangering peace. Six months later he visited Czechoslovakia which still enjoyed democracy and met President Beneš and Klement Gottwald, the Communist Prime Minister, as well as leaders of the Catholic Church. On his return he praised the democracy of the country and must have felt some discomfort when, in February 1948, Gottwald, with Soviet backing, led a coup which brought democracy to an end in that country.

Callaghan continued his foreign travels in December 1946 when as part of the Empire Parliamentary Association he visited Nigeria, the Gold Coast, Gambia and Sierra Leone, the West African colonies of the British Empire. In today's rough and tumble of media coverage which displays an unhealthy disrespect for politics and politicians such trips would be described as 'foreign junkets' but they proved to be useful to Callaghan, establishing contacts with emerging nationalist leaders he found useful when he became Shadow Colonial Secretary in 1957.

In 1947, when Callaghan addressed the Labour Party Conference he emphasised the fact that Britain's African colonies belonged to the Africans. He also understood however that Britain had a responsibility to those countries it had colonised, and could not simply walk away and leave the countries to sink or swim on their own. He argued strongly that economic development would have to go hand in hand with moves towards independence. Such views might today appear to be simple logic and very obvious but in the Britain of the 1950s the British Empire was still a matter of great pride and the ethics of the British ruling over countries in other continents was not questioned, particularly when they were essentially populated by black people unlike Australia, New Zealand or Canada where the indigenous populations were discreetly forgotten. Callaghan's approach to the colonies was radical.

The Cardiff South MP was beginning to attract attention within Parliament and was being talked about as someone who could climb the ladder but to his credit this did not prevent Callaghan from airing his dissent on Government policies. Although not a member of the Keep Left group of Labour MPs, he signed a letter along with 20 other MPs including Michael Foot, Jenny Lee and Richard Crossman calling for a 'socialist foreign policy' which carved a middle way between the raw capitalism of the USA and the totalitarianism of Russia.

Callaghan chaired Labour's Defence and Services Group which condemned the fact that by the end of 1946 there were still 1.3 million men and women in the armed services. Feelings on this issue had been heightened by the fact that in the King's Speech in November 1946 the Government proposed reintroducing conscription for a period of 18 months. When the National Service Bill came before the House on 1 April Labour MPs voted against it and a further 70, including Callaghan, abstained. To assuage the emotions raised by the Bill, the

Richard Crossman, son of a High Court judge, was elected MP for Coventry in 1945 and was appointed Minister of Housing and Local Government in Harold Wilson's first Cabinet in October 1964. He became Leader of the House in 1966 and later Secretary of State for the newly formed Department of Health and Social Security in October 1968. Following Labour's defeat in the June 1970 general election Crossman remained in Parliament but became editor of the *New Statesman*, a position he held until March 1972. He died on 5 April 1974. The publication of his diaries between 1975 and 1977 provoked much controversy and legal attempts were made to prevent their publication.

government reduced the period from 18 to 12 months, a move welcomed by Callaghan in a speech in the Commons.

The crisis which had been predicted in December 1945 when the USA insisted on Sterling becoming convertible came about on 15 July. Callaghan's earlier comments that the terms of the loan amounted to *economic aggression by the United States* were fully justified; indeed it could be argued that they were overly mild as the United Kingdom was enmeshed in a financial crisis which at times appeared to threaten the very existence of the country. The effects in financial terms were of tsunami proportions. There was a tidal wave of dollar reserves pouring out of the country resulting in the stock market plummeting and Britain stared bankruptcy in the face. To add further insult the residue of the loan amounting to $400 million was frozen by the US Treasury. The full impact of what was happening finally dawned in Washington and the convertibility of Sterling was brought to an end on 20 August. In response to the crisis Callaghan's Defence and Services group widened its remit to include the economy and Callaghan as a delegate to the TUC made a speech criticising the government on its handling of the economy.

At the onset of the crisis Callaghan, along with 18 other MPs including Michael Foot, Barbara Castle, Ian Mikardo and George Wigg, addressed a letter to Attlee demanding import controls and for the armed services to be reduced to 600,000 men by the following year. The signatories also called for taxes on capital appreciation and profits while expenditure on housing and social services should be protected. During the committee stage of the Finance Bill Callaghan congratulated Hugh Dalton, the Chancellor of Exchequer on maintaining a high rate of tax on the rich. He took this opportunity to attack the continued distribution of dividends to shareholders at a time when employees were suffering financially.

Despite his various criticisms of the government Callaghan found himself on the first rung of Parliamentary promotion when, in October 1947, Attlee appointed him Parliamentary Secretary to Alfred Bournes, the Minister of Transport. This move came as a minor part of a fairly major reshuffle with Sir Stafford Cripps becoming Minister of Economic Affairs, the departure of Arthur Greenwood from the Cabinet, while Hugh Gaitskell replaced Emmanuel Shinwell at Fuel and Power and Harold Wilson made Cabinet rank with his appointment as President of the Board of Trade.

Callaghan's willingness to voice dissent had obviously not done him much harm but when you examine his actions there is already the pragmatic approach to political issues which was to remain with him throughout his political career. Although he had signed the letter emanating from the Keep Left Group calling for a 'socialist foreign policy', Callaghan was never a member of the group. On the question of conscription Callaghan although criticising the government did not vote against the Bill but only abstained. He also, while signing the letter to Attlee calling for import controls, at the same time praised the Chancellor of Exchequer Hugh Dalton for his actions on several fronts. It is actions such as these which prevented pundits or colleagues in the party putting a label on Callaghan. There is no doubt that he was, in today's terms, a left-wing MP but as has often been said before when attempting to put a left-wing or right-wing label on anyone, it depends the company they are in. Callaghan was a member of the most radical Labour government there ever has been. He was in the mainstream of current political thinking in the immediate post-war Labour Party although if he was to be reincarnated on the political scene today and espouse the same views he would immediately be labelled as far left, if not 'loony' left.

An early indication came in Callaghan's political career that wage control under its many guises was to follow him no matter what government position he held when, while a junior minister in the Ministry of Transport, Britain's major docks were brought to a halt by industrial action. Callaghan had been called by Attlee to Number 10 in October 1947 to be offered the position of Parliamentary Secretary to the Ministry of Transport under Alfred Barnes. Only a few months later Britain faced a major crisis when during a voluntary wage freeze in the summer of 1948 unofficial dock strikes in Liverpool and the Port of London by 16,000 dockers forced Attlee to ask the King to declare a State of Emergency. Callaghan attended the Cabinet's Emergencies Committee chaired by the Home Secretary Chuter Ede. He must have been uneasy at the idea of using troops to break a strike but in his autobiography he makes no reference to opposing the move. There is no doubt that the dispute was extremely damaging to Britain's fragile economy. The populace were still enduring food rationing and the country needed to export to keep afloat. The arrival of the troops on the docksides brought the unofficial strikes quickly to an end but there was still a rumbling of discontent among dockers who felt aggrieved at the system of casual working operated in the docks. Twelve months later industrial action again flared up which resulted in Attlee using the 1920 Emergency Powers Act and again asking the King to declare a State of Emergency. The strike which began in May 1949 finally ended in July after 15,000 troops had been used to unload cargoes. Although ostensibly called in support of Canadian seamen there was the underlying problem of the Dock Labour Board which resulted in dockers working for different master stevedores. Callaghan sympathised with the feelings of the dockers on this issue although he again supported the action taken by the government to break the dispute. However he wrote to Attlee to protest over how the Dock Labour Scheme was operated.

His time at the Ministry of Transport was not totally enmeshed in industrial disputes. Britain's road users, both drivers and pedestrians can thank Callaghan for two highly innovative initiatives which today are taken for granted – zebra crossings and cats'-eyes. Civil servants at the ministry showed Callaghan full-scale models of white lines drawn across the road at pedestrian crossings to make them more visible to motorists and the enthusiastic junior minister set about persuading Alfred Barnes to introduce the markings which quickly became known as zebra crossings. It was also Callaghan who overcame the scepticism of transport officials and introduced cats'-eyes on Britain's main trunk roads.

Callaghan's period at the Ministry of Transport came to an end in February, 1950 when a general election was called. His constituency was renamed Cardiff South and boundary changes meant that it now contained more middle class areas, this coming at a time when Callaghan had upset a sizeable minority of his working class constituents by refusing to support the funding of Catholic schools. Despite these potential problems Callaghan held the seat with a majority of 5,895. His personal victory however was tempered by the fact that Labour's overall majority had been slashed to a mere 10 which called into question how long the new government would be able to hold on to power.

Callaghan was appointed Parliamentary and Financial Secretary to the Admiralty under Viscount Hall who sat in the Lords. This promotion meant Callaghan had the responsibility of speaking on naval matters in the Commons. Callaghan's standing was further enhanced when Hugh Dalton, who had long acted as a mentor to his younger colleague, invited him to act as his deputy on the British delegation to the new Council of Europe. Ten European Governments had agreed to the formation of the Council in May 1949 aimed to achieving more co-operation between the members. This was quickly followed in May 1950 by the Schuman Plan proposed by Jean Monnet to form a European Coal and Steel Community with its primary aim to ensure that no single European power could build an armament industry as their heavy industries would be developed by the new body and not at a national level. This development had the added benefit of allowing Germany to rebuild its industrial base without arousing fears among its neighbours. France, West Germany, Italy and the Benelux countries joined the new economic body. The Schuman Plan was seen as preparing the ground for a future federal structure in Europe and Britain did not join. This view was shared by Callaghan who while supporting economic co-operation was steadfastly against the idea being mooted of a European defence force. Callaghan attended the Council of Europe meeting in Strasbourg mixing with prominent political figures such as Monnet, Mollet, Schuman and Spaak. This was an important step in Callaghan's political education.

At home, Callaghan was not given long to settle into his new ministerial role. His responsibilities included equipping the Senior Service and in March 1950 he rose in the Commons to announce the Naval Estimates for the coming year. Naval manpower was reduced from 153,000 to 143,000 but the *Amethyst* incident in 1949 when the Royal Navy sailed up the Yangtze caused the government to increase expenditure in the Far East as tension between Britain and China now ruled by the Communist Party continued. He also announced a building programme which included six aircraft carriers including the *Eagle* and the *Ark Royal*, the largest carriers in the British fleet.

During his time in the Admiralty British forces supported the USA when the Korean War broke out on 25 June 1950 following the invasion of South Korea by North Korean troops. The UN Security Council called on North Korea to withdraw its troops back to the 38th Parallel, followed by another resolution calling on member states to render what assistance they could to South Korea. The Attlee government agreed to commit troops to this new theatre of war, and British warships along with ships from the US Seventh Fleet took part in the landings at Inchon. The Korean conflict resulted in Britain having to rearm, and despite the economic problems facing the country the government committed themselves to a £3.4 billion rearmament programme over three years. The Navy was allocated £278 million and Callaghan oversaw how this money was spent. The money spent on arms had to be found from other parts of the government budget which led to a major split in Labour's ranks when it was proposed in the April 1951 Budget that charges for dentures and spectacles be introduced in the National Health Service. This led to the resignation of Aneurin Bevan and the formation around him of a group of MPs who became known as 'Bevanites' while another group gave their support to the Chancellor of Exchequer, Hugh Gaitskell and were referred in the media as 'Gaitskellites'. Callaghan again displayed his reluctance to join factions and although more in sympathy with Gaitskell did not join either grouping. Indeed immediately prior to the Budget statement in the Commons Callaghan had tried to persuade Bevan not to resign, but following the Budget both Nye Bevan and Harold Wilson resigned from the Cabinet.

In May 1951 Callaghan had hoped to be promoted to First Lord of the Admiralty following the resignation of Viscount Hall but Attlee gave the job to Frank Pakenham. A few months later in September 1951 Attlee called a general election. Despite the fact that Labour received more votes overall than the Conservatives they lost the election with 295 seats to the Conservative's 321. Callaghan retained his own seat with a majority of 4,499. The defeat of the Labour government was partly brought about by the fact that the party leadership were tired after 11 years in government, although five of these years were as ministers in the wartime National Government.

Losing power resulted in new faces appearing on the Labour Front Bench, among them Callaghan's. He was elected to the Shadow Cabinet, coming a credible seventh of the 12 elected in November 1951. This was to be the start of 29 years on Labour's Front Bench either as a member of the Shadow Cabinet or Cabinet. Initially he was given the Transport portfolio but he still maintained his strong interest in foreign affairs which led Hugh Cudlipp of the *Daily Mirror* sending him as part of the paper's journalistic team to cover the Geneva international conference called to resolve the Indo-China crisis brought about by the French defeat at Dien Bien Phu in May 1954. This assignment gave him the opportunity to watch how figures on the international stage of politics conducted themselves. Taking part were personalities such as the US Secretary of State John Foster Dulles, the Soviet Union's Foreign Minister Vyacheslav Molotov and France's new Prime Minister Pierre Mendes-France as well as Britain's Foreign Secretary Anthony Eden.

It was during these early years in Opposition as a Shadow Minister that Callaghan made his first visit to Northern Ireland at the behest of the Northern Irish TUC and Labour Party in the Province. British governments, no matter their political hue, had shown little interest in this part of the United Kingdom ever since it came into being in 1921 when Ireland was partitioned. The Ulster Unionists were given free rein to govern the Province from Stormont without interference from London. Callaghan was shocked by the level of unemployment he encountered and on his return to London made several speeches on the issue. He called for a development corporation to be established to stimulate the economy but this futuristic concept was not acted upon until many more years of neglect by Britain had passed, leading to widespread disorder and a bloody conflict which was to last 30 years. Callaghan however did not draw attention to the fact that the brunt of the unemployment was borne by the minority Catholic population of the Six Counties. It is difficult to believe that his attention was not drawn to the discriminatory policies carried out by the Protestant ascendancy which had ruled Northern Ireland unbroken for more than 30 years. It must be assumed that the Belfast Harland and Wolff shipyard featured at some point in his visit, yet Callaghan, by now an experienced politician, did not seem aware that few Catholics found employment in its vast sheds. Or, if he was aware, he chose to turn a blind eye and not bring the sectarian problems across the Irish Sea to the UK Parliament, although he did mention some of the problems Catholics encountered in Derry. Northern Ireland remained the untouchable sore of UK life until 1969 when ironically it fell to Jim Callaghan, by then Home Secretary in the Wilson government, to grapple with the legacy of Ulster Unionist misrule.

In May 1955 Anthony Eden, who had succeeded Sir Winston Churchill as Prime Minister the previous month, called a general election following an election budget by Rab Butler featuring a reduction in the standard rate of income tax aimed at keeping the electorate happy. It worked. The Conservatives increased their majority over Labour, winning 345 seats to Labour's 277. Callaghan held his own seat although with a reduced majority of 3,240. Shortly after the election, in November, Attlee resigned as leader of the Labour Party, and Hugh Gaitskell won the subsequent leadership contest with 157 votes to Bevan's 70 and Morrison's 40. Callaghan had campaigned for Gaitskell and in the reshuffle following Gaitskell's victory he became shadow spokesman for fuel and power. The following year in the summer of 1956 he was again moved, this time to education and science. His interest in foreign affairs also led him to being one of Labour's shadow ministers who met with the colourful Soviet leader Nikita Khrushchev during his visit to Britain in April 1956. The meeting discussed the Soviet Union's treatment of dissidents, and was not a diplomatic success. Khrushchev, unhappy at his treatment at the hands of the Labour leadership, later told journalists that if he lived in Britain he would be more attracted to the Conservative Party! The Soviet visitors, who included the Soviet Defence Minister Nikolai Bulganin, stayed at Claridges Hotel during their stay in London and Callaghan attended an important meeting there when he acted as a rapporteur when Harold Strassen, the US representative on the disarmament commission and Sir William Hayter, the British Ambassador to Moscow, met

Great things were expected of Hugh Gaitskell who led the Labour Party from 1955 until January 1963 when he died at the age of 56. He was elected to Parliament as member for Leeds South in 1945, and was Chancellor of Exchequer in Atlee's government in 1950–1 when he caused a storm in Labour ranks by imposing charges for medical and dental treatment. He succeeded Atlee as leader, defeating Bevan by 157 votes to 70. He led the attack in the Commons against Britain's involvement in Suez. Gaitskell was admitted to hospital in November 1962 suffering from a virus. He died unexpectedly on 18 January 1963.

Khrushchev with Malik the Soviet Union's ambassador to Britain to discuss East-West disarmament.

Following the Suez crisis in November 1956, Aneurin Bevan came in from the cold and was appointed shadow spokesman on foreign affairs which led to Callaghan filling Bevan's former position as spokesman on colonial policy, a relatively high-profile position as the 'wind of change' was just gathering force in Britain's African colonies. The Conservative Party was a strong upholder of the Empire. Only two years before Callaghan's appointment as the Labour Party's spokesman on colonial affairs Henry Hopkinson, Colonial Minister of State had declared with the arrogance of a Roman senator that the Mediterranean island of Cyprus was crucial to Britain as an air and naval base and therefore could 'never' expect self-government. It is hardly surprising that faced with such a blunt statement that the following year Colonel Georgios Grivas formed EOKA (National Organisation of Cypriot Struggle). The island's population was divided into two distinct ethnic groups, Greek and Turkish. Archbishop Makarios, the political leader of the Greek Cypriots who accounted for 80 per cent of the population wanted union with Greece. Britain's response was to send him into exile on the remote Seychelles islands in the Indian Ocean. No one in the British Establishment appeared to stop and think that what might have been acceptable when Napoleon was exiled to St Helena was outmoded in the 20th century. Callaghan condemned the decision to send Makarios into exile and warned that partition would not work. Makarios was allowed to return to Cyprus in 1957 and a solution to Britain's difficulties in Cyprus was finally found in 1959, although the problem between the two ethnic groups continues until this day.

But Cyprus was only a microcosm of Britain's colonial

problems. The demand for independence in the African colonies was rapidly reaching a crescendo. The situation in the African colonies had the added problem of a large white population who had left Britain to put roots down in Africa. These white settlers enjoyed a privileged life-style at the expense of the native Africans. They held the reins of power in colonies such as Kenya, Northern Rhodesia (Zambia), Southern Rhodesia (Zimbabwe) and Nyasaland (Malawi). They were not about to voluntarily relinquish their supremacy which was buttressed by racial discrimination policies. The white communities in Africa had many sympathisers and friends in the Conservative Party. This cocktail of pseudo kinship between the ruling classes in the Mother of Parliaments and our African colonies ensured a bumpy ride towards independence in these countries. Callaghan was a vehement opponent of the government's policies towards the African colonies and conducted a vocal and effective campaign both in and outside the Commons against them. There can be little doubt that if Labour had been in power during this period of history the break-up of the Empire in African would have been achieved much more humanely.

In Kenya the 45,000 white settlers enjoyed many privileges including the exclusive use of the fertile highland plateau which Africans were banned from farming. In the early 1950s an armed insurgency, Mau Mau, began which led to a bloody conflict with the British army. Detention camps were established and some 90,000 African men were herded into them. The media in Britain painted a gruesome picture of Mau Mau atrocities but the total number of whites to lose their lives during the four-year conflict was less than 70 compared to thousands of Africans. In 1954 Jomo Kenyatta, leader of the Kenya African National Union, was sentenced to hard labour. Callaghan urged the government to seek a settlement and visited Kenyatta in prison. There was widespread public outrage when it emerged that 11 Kikuyu detainees in the Hola Camp had been beaten to death by their armed guards. Callaghan attacked the government's handling of the affair and called upon the Colonial Secretary Alan Lennox-Boyd to resign. Lennox-Boyd did not respond immediately but shortly afterwards left politics. Callaghan's handling of the affair attracted much praise and enhanced his political reputation.

The Central African Federation of Northern and Southern Rhodesia and Nyasaland was also proving to be a thorn in Britain's relationship with its colonies once again acerbated by the presence of a sizeable white community, particularly in Southern Rhodesia where the 50,000 white population controlled 49 million acres of land compared to the 29 million acres allocated to the country's one million African population. The apartheid-style laws of Southern Rhodesia ensured the political and economic dominance of the white settlers in this country, who saw the formation of the Central African Federation in 1953 as a way of halting African rule in their two neighbouring states. The Federation was governed from Salisbury, the capital of Southern Rhodesia, and the ambition was for the Federation to be granted independence from Britain complete with a constitution which guaranteed continued white rule throughout the Federation. Callaghan led the Opposition benches in the Commons in a determined fight against moves to grant independence to the Federation against the wishes of the African majority and also under a constitution which blatantly discriminated against black Africans.

In September 1957 he was invited by the Commonwealth Parliamentary Association along with other MPs to visit the Federation and heard at first hand the opposition of African leaders to the Constitutional Amendment Bill proposed by the Conservative government. Following his visit Callaghan won Labour Party support for a policy of no independence for the Federation which did not offer black African majority rule. He also said that a future Labour government would wind the Federation up if they could not agree a constitution which recognised the democratic rights of the African population. He condemned the working conditions of black Africans in the copper mines and the lack of education for young black girls.

In November 1957 he opposed the Constitutional Amendment Bill in the Commons as being biased against Africans and called on the British government not to hand power to a Federation government led by Roy Welensky. African leaders such as Kenneth Kaunda in Northern Rhodesia and Hastings Banda in Nyasaland lent their vocal opposition against the Bill. Violent opposition to the Federation's white supremacy began to erupt in the three member states of the Federation in March. This was met by a Law and Order Act which banned even peaceful demonstrations. In mid-1959 Lord Devlin in a report condemned the colonial rule in Nyasaland as being akin to a police state. In the Commons Callaghan called for the acceptance of the Devlin Report. He also called for political detainees to be either brought to trial or released. The deteriorating situation forced the Conservative government to think again and the Monckton Commission was appointed to examine the conditions in the Federation. The findings of the Monckton Commission in October 1960 were to spell the end of any prospect of the white dominated Federation being granted independence. The Commission concluded that there was overwhelming African opposition to the Federation and proposed that there should be a Federation assembly with seats equally divided between Africans and Europeans with a majority of Africans in the governments of Northern Rhodesia and Nyasaland. Callaghan was quick to praise the Commission for its work and called for Joshua Nkomo to be released from imprisonment in Southern Rhodesia. In March 1963 Nyasaland and Northern Rhodesia seceded from the Federation which ceased to exist in January 1964.

Chapter 3: Chancellor of the Exchequer

The British public were enjoying a phoney sense of well-being when the Prime Minister Sir Alec Douglas-Home called a general election for mid-October 1964. Unemployment and inflation were low and there was a general air of affluence around as a result of Reginald Maudling's election-eering Budget decision to reflate the economy by increasing spending on health, housing and education. These measures had helped bring unemployment down and earnings were rising by 9 per cent a year. The economy was expanding at 6 per cent but imports were growing fast and behind the feel-good factor was an approaching balance of payments and Sterling crisis. The Bank of England and many economists had warned that the boom economy was unsustainable. However, the public was largely ignorant of the economic realities and enjoyed the aura of prosperity. This resulted in a narrowing of Labour's lead in the polls and the general election was a hard-fought affair.

Labour gained a net 56 seats, giving them 317 seats in the new Parliament to the Conservative's 303 with the Liberals on 9. The new government was immediately faced with major problems on several fronts. Only 24 hours earlier China had exploded its first nuclear weapon and Khrushchev had been overthrown as Soviet leader to be replaced by Kosygin. Overshadowing all this was the economic situation facing

Britain. The balance of payments for September had just been announced and the Treasury officials were forecasting an annual deficit of £800 million.

Harold Wilson, as the new Prime Minister, acted quickly to appoint Jim Callaghan as Chancellor of Exchequer and George Brown to head the new Department of Economic Affairs (DEA). Wilson met with both men in the evening of 16 October to agree the broad divisions of responsibilities between the two departments although the formal protocols were not agreed until December. Wilson in his book *The Labour Government 1964–70* makes it clear the importance he attached to the Department of Economic Affairs, writing '... Britain could hope to win economic security only by a fundamental reconstruction and modernisation of industry under the direction of a department at least as powerful as the Treasury.'[1]

The new department would be responsible for economic planning and strengthening the country's ability to export while at the same time reducing imports by boosting productivity and increasing Britain's competitiveness at home and abroad. George Brown later successfully argued that prices and incomes should be added to the department's powers. The Treasury would continue to be responsible for government expenditure and taxation as well as foreign exchange and internal monetary management. Agreement may have been reached but this formula was to cause tensions in government for most, if not all, of the relatively short life of the Department of Economic Affairs.

Callaghan immediately started getting to grips with the balance of payments deficit which was predicted to continue into 1965. Sterling was under pressure and after only 10 days as occupier of Number 11 Downing Street Callaghan took the decision to impose a 15 per cent surcharge on imports with the exceptions of foodstuffs and raw material. This action caused uproar throughout continental Europe particularly among Britain's European Free Trade Area (EFTA) partners. This decision was made public at a press conference called by George Brown with Callaghan sitting beside him. In his autobiography Callaghan admitted that the decision could have been handled better. The government in their haste to tackle the balance of payments problem had failed to consult foreign governments. The outcry was so intense that the government had to announce that it was a temporary measure. Callaghan accepted that the surcharge encouraged currency speculators to gamble on the possibility of a Sterling devaluation should there still be a balance of payments problem when the surcharge ended.

On 11 November, Callaghan, in what was effectively his first Budget, announced an increase in the standard rate of income tax of 6d (2.4p), while putting the price of a gallon of petrol up by the same amount and introducing a Capital Gains Tax, actions which most economists deemed to be sensible to take the heat out of the economy but the international bankers were displeased. The cause of their displeasure was the social measures the new Chancellor announced. In line with the Labour government's manifesto commitments Callaghan introduced measures to help the lower income groups by increasing the state pension as well as the widow's pension. He also abolished the earnings rule relating to widows' pensions which had meant that for every one shilling (5p) a widow earned over £8 she lost the same amount from her pension. Understandably Callaghan had strong personal views on this subject having watched his mother suffer penury following the death of his father, only partially eased when she was awarded a pension. These socially-motivated measures were frowned upon by the City and the Swiss bankers who immediately began to speculate against Sterling. There was a run on the pound with the reserves being depleted by as much as £50 million a day. It was decided to increase the Bank Rate by 2 per cent to 7 per cent on 23 November, a decision which Callaghan found personally difficult to make. It must have been galling for him to sit on Labour's front bench and listen to the Conservative opposition blame his Budget and the surcharge on imports for the crisis when it was their reckless pursuit of growth in the run up to the general election which lay at the root of the difficulties now facing the government. Handling the crisis was made even more difficult by the attitude adopted by Lord Cromer, Governor of the Bank of England, who consistently argued against the policies on which Labour had been elected. The situation became so serious that in a meeting with Cromer attended by Callaghan Wilson threatened to call a general election and explain that the City and international currency speculators were attempting to dictate to a democratically elected government what policies they could adopt. Shortly after this confrontation, on 25 November the Governor of the Bank of England informed Callaghan and the Prime Minister that he had raised a $3,000 million loan from central bankers with the support of the USA. This gave Sterling a valuable breathing space but the underlying cause of Britain's economic problems remained. Production at home had to be increased not only to increase exports but also to help reduce imports. Sterling still faced difficulties but the loan at least meant that they had the reserves to defend the currency.

Callaghan gave his first traditional Budget speech on 6 April 1965 and although most of the content had already been made in his Ways and Means speech the previous year on 11 November he also announced that the TSR2 strike aircraft project was being scrapped and that the introduction of Corporation Tax would be delayed until April 1966.

The Budget's main thrust was to deflate the economy, reducing Home demand by some £250 million. Although it was criticised by many in the City it did not adversely affect Sterling. Callaghan's prestige rose but the underlying problems remained, and were not to go away. However at the end of May it was agreed that the Bank Rate should be cut from what was viewed as an emergency rate of 7 per cent to 6 per cent. This was accompanied by the tightening-up of hire purchase regulations to reduce domestic consumer spending. The calm on the financial front did not last for long.

In June Callaghan made his first visit to America as Chancellor. The visit was promoted publicly as merely aimed at the strengthening of Britain's transatlantic ties but the main business was to ensure American support for Sterling if there was renewed pressure. Callaghan met Robert MacNamara, the US Defence Secretary, Joe Fowler, Secretary to the Treasury and President Johnson in the White House. The first pressure on Sterling was indeed dealt with thanks to assistance of the USA and the IMF, but the uncertainty still continued partly encouraged by the belief that Wilson would be forced to call a general election leading to a change of government which would be more amenable to devaluation. In an attempt to remove this uncertainty Wilson, in a speech in Glasgow at the end of June, said that he had no intention of calling a general election during 1965. He pointed out that despite having only a parliamentary majority of three the government had still managed to get their Finance Bill through Parliament. The speech however had little effect overseas and the pound started to come under extreme pressure in July.

This forced Callaghan and Wilson to come up with a raft of harsh measures to demonstrate to the international financial community that they were determined to control the economy. Following a Cabinet meeting on 26 July at which the measures were agreed somewhat reluctantly, Callaghan made a statement to the Commons outlining further action to be taken by the government. These were difficult decisions for the Labour movement to swallow both inside and outside Parliament. The starting dates for all government building projects with the exception of housing, industries and hospitals were to be delayed for six months. The government also promised to act to ensure that nationalised industries and local authorities would follow their example. Local authority mortgage lending was cut back. The length of hire-purchase agreements were reduced from three years to 30 months and government plans for earnings-related pensions were postponed. However unpalatable they may have been, Sterling improved following their announcement. The alternative was either to allow the pound to float or to devalue, and it was this debate which was now feeding the pressure on Sterling as speculators around the world were selling Sterling on the assumption that the currency would eventually be devalued.

Callaghan and Wilson had taken a firm stance against devaluation. They were no doubt motivated by the fate of the Labour governments who had devalued the currency in 1931 and 1949. There were a number of Cabinet ministers who did not share this view and pressure within government for devaluation to be at least seriously considered was growing.

As the country fought for its economic survival on an almost day-to-day basis George Brown's DEA announced a five-year plan in September aimed at achieving an annual growth rate of 3.8 per cent covering the period 1964–70. Callaghan publicly supported the plan although he privately harboured doubts about its achievability. There were tensions between the Treasury and the DEA which Callaghan had foresaw and under the leadership of George Brown the DEA was attempting to claim supremacy over its rival departments such as the Treasury and the Board of Trade.

To add to the government's economic woes Ian Smith, the Prime Minister of Southern Rhodesia, declared UDI on 11 November 1965. Although not directly affecting his department Callaghan had tried his best to prevent such action during his period as Shadow Spokesman for Colonial Affairs. He was however involved in the proposed economic sanctions to imposed on the Salisbury government and the freezing of the assets of the Bank of Rhodesia. Wilson also called on him for his advice in dealing with Kenneth Kaunda, President of Zambia (Northern Rhodesia) with whom Callaghan was friendly with.

Labour had struggled valiantly with a slender majority but by the beginning of 1966 the government's majority had been reduced to one. On 28 February Wilson formally announced that there were would be a general election on 31 March but in the intervening period there was a 'little Budget' on 1 March, St David's Day, when Jim Callaghan added a little colour to the occasion by wearing a Welsh daffodil. One of the historic decision's Callaghan made that day was to announce that Britain would go decimal during 1971 bringing an end to the traditional pounds, shillings and pence. Instead the pound would be divided into 100 new pence – no more sixpences, shillings or half crowns. More immediately the Treasury introduced a mortgage-option scheme which would allow home buyers to either pay the full mortgage rate and

'He {Callaghan} is an extremely interesting example of how important image is in modern politics. He has a good public image outside Parliament, his presence in Parliament is exactly right, his personality on TV is just right and he also has a good image in his own department in the sense that they like him.'

RICHARD CROSSMAN

claim tax relief or opt to forego tax relief and pay 2 per cent less than the full mortgage rate. This benefited the lower-paid mortgage holder who did not pay the standard rate of tax and proved to be a popular measure. He also gave details of subsidies for low income earner-ratepayers. At the same time he introduced a tax on betting and gaming.

In his published diaries Richard Crossman, not renowned for his high regard for Callaghan, was fulsome in his praise of the Chancellor. He wrote of Callaghan's Budget speech: 'He did it magnificently with enormous parliamentary skill ... On the TV in the evening he was equally superb. He is an extremely interesting example of how important image is in modern politics. He has a good public image outside Parliament, his presence in Parliament is exactly right, his personality on TV is just right and he also has a good image in his own department in the sense that they like him.' However, Crossman could not help but add: 'The place where he has no reputation at all is in Cabinet where in decision-making with his colleagues he is weak and self-commiserating.'[2]

Labour won 363 seats compared to 253 seats for the Conservatives and the Liberals 12. The new Labour government had an overall majority of 97. The euphoria following Labour's 1966 general election victory was relatively short-lived. It lasted long enough for Callaghan to introduce his Budget on 4 May. He had informed the House that he planned to bring a fuller Budget to the House when he had made his 'little Budget' speech immediately prior to the Election.

The main content of Callaghan's Budget was the introduction of Selective Employment Tax which was heavier on service industries than on manufacturing. Before Callaghan had sat down the speculators had started to sell Sterling. In his autobiography, Callaghan wrote that he believed that one of the reasons for the adverse reaction was the fact that he left news of the Selective Employment Tax to the end by which time the news tapes disseminating his Budget speech around the world had indicated that he was not raising taxes and the reaction had set in.

Twelve days later the National Union of Seamen (NUS) called a national strike and the problems facing Sterling were multiplied. The strike lasted for seven weeks but the drain on the country's reserves was halted by the world's central bankers coming to the rescue with a billion-pound credit package. The NUS strike ended on 1 July but the pressure on Sterling continued into July. On 12 July the pound fell to its lowest point since November 1964. The Balance of Payments deficit was increasing, not helped by the seamen's strike, and looking ahead the £3,385 million loan from the Swiss banks was due to be paid by the end of 1967. The Bank Rate was increased to 7 per cent on 14 July and the government indicated that further measures would be announced later in the month.

Wilson revealed the proposed cuts on 20 July. Callaghan had drawn up a ten-point emergency package to deal with the crisis including the tightening of hire-purchase controls; a 10 per cent hike on alcohol, oil, petrol and purchase taxes; postal charge increases; 10 per cent increase on surtax; reduction on overseas expenditure and the introduction of a limit of £50 travel allowance on tourists travelling outside the Sterling area. The toughest measure introduced by the government was a six-month freeze on wages, salaries and dividend increases.

The measures had been discussed at a Cabinet meeting on 19 July when devaluation was raised for the first time since 1964 as a method of dealing with the pressure on Sterling by Deputy Prime Minister George Brown who also raised the prospect of his resignation during the meeting. Six Cabinet members favoured devaluation but the remaining members favoured the package proposed by the Chancellor. Callaghan wished to make the announcement to the Commons but Wilson insisted that he would make it. The measures succeeded in halting the flow of funds out of Sterling but there was little sign of an inflow.

One of Callaghan's prime worries concerning public expenditure was the amount being spent in the defence budget. To help tackle this he travelled to Bonn to meet Dr Dahlgrin, the West German Finance Minister to discuss West Germany's contribution towards the expenditure on Britain's 60,000 troops deployed in the country. The cost to the British Exchequer was £90 million a year but during the talks the German Finance Minister was only willing to contribute £54 million to which Callaghan replied that Britain would reduce its service personnel by 20,000. In the end a face-saving decision was made to set up a joint committee to look at the problem.

The mercurial George Brown was transferred from the DEA to the Foreign Office early in August, ostensibly to prepare for Britain's application to join the European Common Market. The more mild-mannered Michael Stewart took over at the DEA and Callaghan believed that relations between the Treasury and the DEA would improve as a result. However, a newspaper interview with William Davis of the *Guardian* threw a spanner in the works. During the interview Callaghan indicated that he believed two years at the Treasury was long enough for anyone, and when Davis subsequently asked if the Foreign Office would be of interest, Callaghan replied in positive terms. It was not acceptable that a government minister should appear to be angling for a particular position, certainly not in public. Callaghan himself in his memoirs admits that this was a mistake and describes the chill which developed in his relationship with the Prime Minister. If Crossman is to be believed in his diaries, the chill was more like a Siberian winter.

Relating how he himself was given the position of Lord President in the Cabinet reshuffle which had involved Brown and Stewart moving, Crossman describes how Wilson had remarked that 'the only person who was not going to have a change of office was the person who had gone to William Davis of the *Guardian* and got him to write about his wish to be given the Foreign Office.'[3] Crossman quoted Wilson as saying: 'What I have done this time is to surround myself with friends and isolate Callaghan. When people see the result of what I have done they will realise he has been defeated. Only he doesn't realise it yet.'[4]

This is one example of Wilson's growing paranoia. He was convinced that while he was attending the Moscow Trade Fair in July that there had been a plot by Cabinet members to remove him from office. He had become increasingly obsessed by the concept that he was surrounded by plotters and had immediately read the worse into the *Guardian* article. This was more than likely the reason why, when he appointed Stewart to the DEA position, he had made it public that this department's role would remain untouched despite the fact that he knew that Callaghan was unhappy at the overlapping of responsibilities with the Treasury which often led to delays in decision-making. Callaghan sought a meeting with Wilson at the beginning of September to make clear his unhappiness at the relationship between the Treasury and the DEA. He made no headway and eventually threatened to resign. Wilson however talked him round. Later Wilson promised to have another look at the concordat setting out the responsibilities of the two departments.

The Rhodesian crisis was taking up a great deal of the

government's time. Callaghan at the outset of UDI had favoured a more robust approach to Ian Smith and his fellow rebels including the possible use of force but when the long-term strategy of economic embargoes was adopted he accepted that the time for threat of military action had passed. He was a member of the Rhodesian X committee, the highly secret government group which formulated strategy towards Rhodesia. There was a highly charged meeting of the Commonwealth governments in London. Twenty-two members of the Commonwealth were present with only Tanzania boycotting the meeting. There were several calls for armed force to be used but after days of heated debate the final communiqué backed Britain taking the issue to the United Nations' Security Council seeking backing for mandatory sanctions against Rhodesia. In December 1966 Wilson met Ian Smith for abortive talks on board HMS *Tiger* in the Straits of Gibraltar.

We are back on course. The ship is picking up speed. The economy is moving. Every seaman knows the command at such a time, steady as she goes.

CALLAGHAN

The economic indicators were positive as 1967 began. The Balance of Payments was moving into equilibrium while the Bank Rate was reduced to 6 per cent in March. Callaghan's April Budget was, following Treasury advice, very much a neutral one, the one item of note being the lifting of the 15 per cent surcharge on imports. During his speech Callaghan resorted to naval parlance to describe the state of the British economy. He told MPs: *We are back on course. The ship is picking up speed. The economy is moving. Every seaman knows the command at such a time, steady as she goes.*[5] At the time the media claimed that the Prime Minister was unhappy at not being consulted by the Chancellor and in his diaries Crossman stated that Wilson had told him that the Chancellor had never discussed the Budget with him or shown him a draft until it was too late to do anything. At the Parliamentary Labour Party meeting to discuss the Budget the following day, Crossman claimed that Wilson said to him: 'I wouldn't mind seeing him go. I wouldn't mind at all seeing him go this summer.'[6] This is completely at odds with what Harold Wilson himself says in his *The Labour Government 1964–70* when he stated: 'Jim Callaghan, again keeping me fully informed about his assessment and proposals, accepted the Treasury's advice that no fundamental changes were needed following the action taken the previous July.'[7] One of them was telling porkies or, at least, is being 'economical with the truth'. The Budget went down well with the City and Sterling rose to its full exchange rate of $2.80 to the dollar, for the first time since 1966. Callaghan had reason to be content, but the feeling was not to last for very long.

On 30 April the Cabinet agreed by 13 to 8 that Britain should apply for membership of the Common Market but the bid was short-lived as on 16 May President de Gaulle once again vetoed the application. This setback did not affect Sterling however, and the bank rate was reduced to 5.5 per cent but once again events outside the control of government were looming. Trouble had started brewing in the Middle East in the middle of May when President Nasser began moving troops and supplies close to the Israeli border. At the same time he demanded that the United Nations troops stationed in the Gaza Strip be withdrawn. He also declared that the Straits of Tiran would be closed to Israeli shipping. War broke out on 5 June when Israel warplanes attacked Egypt and their ground forces swept across the desert to the Suez Canal and captured the West Bank, Gaza and East Jerusalem. The Arab countries immediately accused British aircraft of taking part on the Israeli side and the Suez Canal was closed. Britain was also faced with an oil embargo from countries such as Kuwait and Iraq, forcing the country to buy oil from more distant sources thus pushing up the price of oil and having a disastrous effect on the balance of payments.

While still grappling with the problems of the Middle East, the economy was hit in mid-September with a dock strike in Hull, London, Liverpool and Manchester which dragged on for more than eight weeks. Again this had an adverse affect on the balance of payments although Callaghan in his autobiography explained how the adverse affects were magnified by a quirk of bookkeeping which suggested that our exports had collapsed. He explained: *Cargoes waiting to be unloaded from the ships at the quayside were regarded as having been already delivered, and were debited to our overseas account. But conversely, the British goods waiting at the dockside to be sent abroad were regarded as not having been exported and so were not credited.*[8] Callaghan admits that he was not aware of this convention so is not overly critical of the pundits or the foreign exchange dealers who made pessimistic assumptions about Britain's underlying export performances which, when the strike was over, proved to be incorrect, but by that time it was too late. The run on Sterling had begun, and this time it was to end in devaluation of the pound, and in the resignation of Callaghan as Chancellor. Sterling had weathered the Six Day War, the closure of the Suez Canal and the oil embargo but the eight-week dockers' strike further distorted the balance of payments position.

The cumulative effect of these events was to renew pressure on Sterling but the final blow which introduced the spectre of devaluation into the equation was comments made by leading French politicians. The dock strike had adversely affected the October 1967 trade figures and Sterling began to slide, forcing the government to increase the bank rate to 6 per cent in the middle of the month. There then followed a Common Market report which suggested that the pound could not be sustained as a reserve currency. The French Foreign Minister Couve de Murville seized on the report as an opportunity to enter the fray stating that Sterling must become a national, instead of being an international currency before Britain would be ready to enter the EEC. He also hinted that the pound would have to be devalued. This further weakened Sterling and the crisis deepened. Devaluation had been a taboo subject in government circles since Labour had won the 1964 general election when Wilson and Callaghan firmly declared their opposition towards any move to devalue the currency. Their attitude succeeded in removing the question of devaluation from the debate as to how Britain resolved its balance of payments problem. However, it was now re-emerging and was being debated openly in the media with the help of a number of economists who were suggesting that it was inevitable.

Callaghan and Leslie O'Brien, Governor of the Bank of England, maintained an upbeat approach to the problems facing the financial stability of the country. Both spoke at the annual bankers' dinner at the Mansion House on 26 October and gave an optimistic picture of the economy pointing out that if it had not been for the closure of the Suez Canal and the slowing down of the world economy Britain would have achieved a balance of payments surplus in 1967. Pundits interpreted these speeches as flagging up that devaluation was not on the government's agenda and Wilson in his biography confirmed this, but not for long.

The situation was to change rapidly and dramatically when rumours of impending devaluation of Sterling began to circulate among the members of the EEC. A finance committee of the EEC went so far as to place on the agenda for their next meeting in mid-November an item to discuss what members of the EEC should do in the event of Britain devaluing. This had a devastating affect on Sterling which was sold heavily on the international money markets. At the same time Callaghan had a private meeting with Alec Cairncross, the Glaswegian head of the government's Economic Section, who bluntly stated that the value of Sterling could not be maintained. In his view, devaluation was inevitable and should be done as soon as possible. Coming from such a respected figure on whom he had often relied on for advice, this was shattering news for Callaghan. He confided in the Prime Minister that he now harboured doubts that Sterling could be saved. This prompted a frenzy of meetings and telephone calls between British and American representatives and European banks. The international community were left in no doubt that only by committing long-term to the defence of Sterling could a global financial crisis be averted.

If the battle to save the pound was lost then Jim Callaghan would resign as Chancellor. He informed the Prime Minister of his intention at a meeting between them on 8 November. Wilson told Callaghan that he would refuse to accept his resignation as it was the policy of the government to defend the pound and not that of any one minister. The IMF offered a contingency fund of $3 billion but with stringent conditions attached which Wilson and Callaghan believed would allow the IMF to dictate or interfere in economic policy. This offer was rejected and although there were efforts to soften the IMF stance this line of defence came to nothing. The Cabinet had agreed that the only way devaluation could be avoided was if the international community accepted that the devaluation of Sterling was not in anyone's interests and committed themselves to the long-term defence of Sterling. They made it clear that they were not interested in borrowing more money on a crisis to crisis basis. Callaghan and other ministers had begun to prepare the detailed package that would be introduced if devaluation proved impossible to avoid.

On Wednesday 15 November the historic decision was taken by the Cabinet, committing the government to devaluing unless there was a last-minute change in circumstances. A group of ministers consisting of the Chancellor, Foreign Secretary, Defence Secretary, the President of the Board of Trade and First Secretary had been preparing the groundwork. The decision was taken to announce their decision to devalue on Saturday 18 November with a new fixed rate of $2.40 to the pound, a 14.3 per cent reduction from its existing rate of $2.80.

The announcement was made at 9.30 p.m. on Saturday evening. At the same time it was announced that the Bank Rate would be increased to 8 per cent. Hire purchase regulations on cars were tightened requiring purchasers to pay a minimum deposit of 33.5 per cent with a maximum repayment period of 27 months. Defence expenditure was to be cut by £100 million. Expenditure on the nationalised industries would be reduced by £100 million. A further £100 million was to be saved by withdrawing SET repayments except in development areas and the export rebate introduced in 1964 was abolished providing almost another £100 million of savings. Corporation Tax was increased from 40 to 42.5 per cent. It was also announced that the government would be seeking a new IMF stand-by arrangement of $1.4 billion. Banks and the Stock Exchange were to be closed on Monday, 20 November.

Crossman in his diaries was highly critical of how both the Prime Minister and Callaghan dealt with the issue, and both men in their autobiographies directed some sharp words in the direction of Crossman. Wilson wrote: 'At Friday night's meeting of ministers and my private office staff on the eve of devaluation I was pressed, above all by Dick Crossman to alter the tone of the broadcast, and to drop the references to set-back and defeat, and almost to exult in our decision. I believe I was wrong to accept this advice and a comparison today of my original draft with the text of my Sunday broadcast suggests that I should have stuck to my first thoughts',[9] while Callaghan wrote: *Dick Crossman offered the Prime Minister ungenerous and ill-timed advice on the stance he should take. He wrote 'Jim must be the Chamberlain of our times and you the Churchill.' I blame him for the fact that Harold's first post-devaluation press conference struck a false note.*[10]

In the build-up to the devaluation announcement Callaghan was faced with a tricky situation when the Labour backbencher Robert Sheldon tabled a motion concerning the rumour of Britain receiving a loan from banks. Callaghan was in a quandary. He did not wish to lie to the Commons but at the same time it would be financially disastrous for the country if the government's decision to announce the devaluation of the pound was to be made public before 18 November. Callaghan replied to the initial question saying that he did not comment on rumours. It was however a follow-up question from Stan Orme suggesting that devaluation was preferable to deflation which was to cause major problems for Sterling. Callaghan replied that he had nothing to *add or subtract from, anything I have said on previous occasions on the subject of devaluation ...* The speculators seized on the fact that the Chancellor had not taken the opportunity to deny that there would be any devaluation and began to sell Sterling. The flight from Sterling meant £1,500 million was lost in the next 24 hours. The blame for the renewed run on Sterling and the financial losses was laid at the Chancellor's door. There were those in the Cabinet who believed that he should have simply denied that devaluation was on the cards. In the light of these criticisms at the time it is ironic that many years later in 1994 Callaghan was accused of lying to the Commons. The Conservative minister William Waldegrave told the Commons Treasury and Civil Service Select Committee that Ministers sometimes had to lie to the House of Commons because of reasons of state. Waldegrave was at the time accused of misleading Parliament over the sale of arms to Iraq and told the Committee that this is what Callaghan had done at the time of devaluation. Callaghan was upset at his integrity being questioned and raised the matter with Waldegrave and John Major who was Prime Minister. Major replied saying that Callaghan had acted 'entirely properly' during the devaluation episode and several Conservatives also sided with Callaghan. It should be recognised that Callaghan was in a very difficult position when faced with such a question. The Cabinet had made a decision but it would have caused untold damage if this had been made public while the money markets around the world were still open. He was also trying not to lie to the Commons.

The Prime Minister made a broadcast on Sunday 19 November in which he said that devaluation 'does not mean that the pound in your pocket is worth 14 per cent less to us now than it was this [i.e. Saturday] morning.' Labour's political opponents jumped on this phrase and accused the Prime Minister of misleading the British people that prices would not rise as a result of devaluation. These accusations rankled with Wilson who elsewhere in his statement had made it clear that some prices would rise but that every effort would be made to keep these to the minimum. The devaluation process had gone well, with only Ireland, New Zealand and Denmark following Britain and devaluing their own currencies which meant that Britain could expect to benefit from the lower cost of her exports.

This did not change Callaghan's mind regarding resignation. Immediately after devaluation was announced he pressed Wilson to accept his resignation as Chancellor. He felt that he had given people, including some heads of state, unequivocal assurances that the currency would not be devalued and as a result they had continued to hold Sterling resulting in financial losses for their countries.

On 30 November 1967, Wilson transferred Callaghan to the Home Office while Roy Jenkins moved in the other direction to become Chancellor of the Exchequer. There has been criticism of Callaghan's period as Chancellor, particularly of his refusal to consider devaluation at an earlier date. Few would claim that Callaghan was a five-star Chancellor but he was not alone in his opposition to devaluation. The *Financial Times* in its published history, *The Financial Times, A Centenary History* quotes from the paper's leader column of 23 November 1964 during the Sterling crisis which followed Callaghan's first Budget as Chancellor of Exchequer: 'Confidence has been shaken and there is sporadic talk of devaluation again. This is silly stuff in itself. Britain's deficit has not suddenly become larger than it was; it is generally agreed in fact that it will be considerably smaller in 1965 ... There can be no question of a forced devaluation ... No Labour Government is likely to contemplate incurring for the second time the odium of such a step.'[11]

It took the conservative-minded *FT* almost as long as the Labour government to come round to the belief that devaluation was perhaps the only answer. Their centenary history had this to say concerning the events of 1967: 'The paper itself, as it became clear that the measures of July 1966 had not worked, at last began publicly to take on board the possibility that devaluation might be a lesser evil than another huge foreign loan.'[12] On Friday 17 November 1967 the main leader argued that 'we would do better to take whatever steps are necessary to put the balance of payments straight by ourselves since previous loans have allowed the government to put off the moment of truth when the need to get out of deficit at least becomes clear.'[13]

The *FT* accused the Labour government of failure for having to devalue and debunked claims that it had been blown off course by events which no one could have foreseen. Looking at the situation which developed in the lead up to devaluation dispassionately it is difficult to understand how anyone can argue that the Six Day War, closure of the Suez Canal, a dockers' strike and unhelpful statements and actions in Europe could not have had serious repercussions on the balance of payments and ultimately the value of Sterling. At the same time it is difficult to imagine how any government could have foreseen such events and therefore take action to alleviate their effects.

Callaghan has been accused of never being fully in control of the economy during his term as Chancellor but it should be remembered that he had to cope with the new Department of Economic Affairs under George Brown. He also came into office in 1964 with a massive £800-million deficit caused by the previous Conservatives' boom-bust economic policies. During his period at the helm to use his favoured navy parlance style, he announced the timetable for decimalisation, introduced Capital Gains Tax, reduced our annual balance of payments deficit and maintained low unemployment. He must also be given the credit for devising the Special Drawing Rights facility at the IMF which was to prove useful to this organisation in following years in its dealings with financial crisis in various parts of the world. Despite the tribulations he was experiencing as Chancellor, Callaghan took another important step towards his rise to the pinnacle of British politics, He was elected Labour Party Treasurer in October 1967 in a contest against Michael Foot gaining 4.3 million votes to Foot's 2 million at the Labour Party Conference. He was to hold this office until becoming Prime Minister in April 1976 and there can be little doubt that being Party Treasurer played a major role in further increasing his stature within Labour.

Chapter 4: Home Secretary

Crisis appeared to follow Jim Callaghan around. His first crisis was already brewing by the time he arrived at the Home Office in December 1967. Kenyan Asians were arriving in Britain in ever-increasing numbers. In the three months ending January 1968 7,000 had arrived, more than in the whole of 1966. When Kenya became independent in December 1963 the Asian residents of Kenya, who mainly originated from India, were given the opportunity to become Kenyan citizens. They were also guaranteed a British passport on request. The same applied in Uganda and Tanzania. In all some 300,000 Asians in the three countries opted to remain British, 40,000 of these in Kenya. In December 1967 President Jomo Kenyatta announced that Kenyan residents who were not citizens would be required to apply for 'entry certificates' despite the fact that the vast majority of Asians had been born there. This resulted in an exodus of Asians from the country using their right to a British passport to come to Britain. The sheer numbers presented the government with a problem.

The Home Office had already been considering what steps to take to stem the flow of immigrants before Callaghan arrived but no action had been taken. Callaghan believed that the situation had to be tackled urgently as up to 300 immigrants were arriving at London airport every day. The media presented this influx as Britain being swamped by immigrants. In his biography Callaghan denied that the country was in danger of being swamped but said that the media coverage had heightened fear and tensions within communities. He asserted that the only way to deal with this was to present a Bill which gave the public the reassurance that immigration was being effectively controlled.

He presented his Commonwealth Immigrants Bill to the Cabinet. In his memoirs he claimed that this Bill would fulfil Britain's obligations to everyone who was entitled to come to Britain and that the government would establish a register of all those who wished to come and issue a specific number of entry vouchers on an annual basis so that they would arrive here in a controlled manner. He also claimed that the Bill would result in the allocation of 5,500 vouchers to heads of families in the first year and that together with surplus vouchers not taken up by other parts of the Commonwealth, he expected there would be enough vouchers to allow around 30,000 Asians into Britain in the first 12 months. These benign figures are not reflected in Harold Wilson's recollection of the Bill as he states in his biography that it would have limited 'the number of special vouchers to be issued to them to 1,500 a year'.[1] Callaghan was upset by accusations of racism but the fact is that the Bill was overtly racial in its content as it stated that the restrictions did not apply to passport holders who could prove 'a substantial connection with the United Kingdom', a coded reference to white settlers. In his biography Callaghan describes the provision in the Westminster Statute which granted Kenya and Uganda their independence allowing inhabitants of the former colonies the entitlement to a British passport as a 'loophole'. This provision, Callaghan believed, was aimed at safeguarding the rights of British settlers but had not specified this, thus giving the right to a British passport to Asian Kenyans. The

Cabinet agreed and the Bill was passed by the Commons on 1 March 1968. The Conservatives had helped ease its passage by not opposing it. Two years later in 1970 the European Commission on Human Rights condemned the policy as racially discriminatory. Around the same time Callaghan also introduced a Race Relations Bill which among other things established a Race Relations Board. This Bill laid down that discrimination on grounds of race in employment or housing was illegal and a Community Relations Commission was formed to investigate any complaints.

Another area which Roy Jenkins had been working on before his transfer to the Treasury was how young people in trouble should be dealt with. Callaghan took this over and in May 1968 published a white paper, *Children in Trouble*, which proposed that a child under 14 should not be taken to court unless he or she was clearly beyond the control of their parents. These measures became law in the Children and Young Persons Act in 1969.

One of the main responsibilities of a Home Secretary is handling the police, and Callaghan seemed better suited than most for this part of the job as he had a very successful period as parliamentary consultant to the Police Federation between 1955 and 1964. The anti-Vietnam War movement planned a major demonstration ending in a rally in Hyde Park. The media predicted that this demonstration would lead to widespread violence and the Opposition called for Callaghan to ban the march and for troops to be put on standby. But Callaghan, working on the basis of 'freedom under the law', rejected these calls, having had discussions with the Metropolitan Police who were confident that they had learned the lessons from a previous demonstration held in the summer. Prior to the demonstration the Home Secretary had been warned that a minority Maoist group taking part planned to lead a breakaway from the main body and attempt to storm the American embassy in Grosvenor Square but the police assured Callaghan that they would be able to handle this. Callaghan adopted a hands-on approach to the demonstration and early in the morning visited the Embankment where the marchers were setting off. His decision to allow the march to take place was totally vindicated. There was some violence by those involved in the breakaway but this was quickly controlled by the police without any major incidents. Following the end of the demonstration Callaghan visited Grosvenor Square where he congratulated the police for their handling of the event. It was a major victory for Callaghan and he was praised in the media for his handling of the situation. His political stock was once again on the rise.

But his relationship with the 'bobby on the beat' did not continue to improve. During 1968 the Federation complained that the wages of their members were falling behind but Callaghan took the view that, since, at the beginning of the 1960s when he was their parliamentary consultant, they had accepted arbitration as a method of resolving pay disputes, they had to accept the findings of the tribunals. Police recruitment was also falling as a result of the public expenditure cuts following devaluation. Callaghan's relationship with the police deteriorated to the extent that the Federation compiled a dossier of complaints against him including the retention of numbers on police uniforms to assist members of the public complaining of police harassment and that police officers might also face penal sanctions if found guilty of racial discrimination. The ill-feeling came to a peak when Callaghan was booed at the Police Federation's annual conference in Llandudno in 1970. His relationship with some elements in the police had not been helped by his opposition to the re-introduction of the death penalty in December 1969. Capital punishment had been abolished in December 1964 by Sydney Silverman's Murder (Abolition of Death) Penalty Bill by 355 votes to 170 but the Lords had amended it to limit its application for five years which meant that it had to be brought back to the Commons. The issue was debated on 16 December 1969 and Callaghan, who had intimated that he would resign as Home Secretary rather than sanction an execution, spoke in favour of abolition. There was a free vote and the abolition of the death penalty was made permanent by 343 to 185.

Traditionally, trade union agreements in Britain had been negotiated at national level but during the 1960s this convention was changing. Plant-level negotiations were becoming much more common and nine out of ten days lost due to industrial action were as a result of unofficial strikes at local level. In 1965 Ray Gunter at the Ministry of Labour had established the Royal Commission on Trade Unions and Employers Associations under the chairmanship of Lord Donovan to examine this problem. The Commission, which became known as the Donovan Commission, reported in June 1968 and crucially came down against using the law to deal with union-management relations. The Commission suggested that companies with plant-level agreements should register with the Department of Employment and Productivity who would lay down rules governing pay negotiations covering dispute procedures and the role of shop stewards but they ruled out using the law as a deterrent against unofficial disputes.

Following the publication of the Commission's report, Barbara Castle as Minister for Employment immediately entered into talks with both sides of industry to take the report forward, and forward she did take it. However she did not accept the Commission's view on legal sanctions. Backed by Harold Wilson she put together a package of industrial relation reforms, some of which were legally enforceable. Her

Cabinet colleagues first heard the details of *In Place of Strife* at a Cabinet meeting on 3 January 1969. The government was to have powers to enforce a ballot before an official strike. The minister would be able to impose a 28-day delay of strike action to allow for conciliation and also to order unofficial strikers back to work with the threat of fines if the order was not obeyed. To oversee industrial relations an Industrial Relations Commission would be established. To sugar these bitter pills, legislation would be introduced to give workers the right to join a union and to give statutory protection against unfair dismissal. The White Paper got off to a bad start as details of the document had been made public after Wilson had briefed the TUC at a meeting on December 30, but before the Cabinet had seen them.

At the Cabinet meeting Callaghan immediately voiced his outright opposition to the proposals; this was to be the start of a six-month Cabinet battle which brought the Home Secretary into direct conflict with the Prime Minister, resulting in calls for Callaghan to resign from the Cabinet. Callaghan did not believe that the law should intervene in trade union affairs, a view he had held from his days as Assistant Secretary of the IRSF. Callaghan had spelled out the reasons when addressing the Fire Brigades Union in May 1968 before the Donovan report was published. He told the delegates: *Self-government is always better than government from above and I have no doubt those solutions to industrial and economic problems which are propounded by the unions themselves and accepted by the democratic decision of its individual members will be more lasting than government intervention.*[2]

The White Paper was published on 17 January and immediately came under sustained attack from the trade union movement. The strength of feeling was shown when Clive Jenkins, General Secretary of the Supervisory Staffs, addressed the Scottish TUC at their Congress in Rothesay, Isle of Bute, in April. Referring to the government's invitation to unions to put alternatives forward, Jenkins said: '... it is rather like being invited to take a hand in the construction of a scaffold and being offered the privilege of tipping the headsman'.[3] Within the trade union movement *In Place of Strife* quickly became known as 'Increase in Strife', which it certainly did. Protest strikes took place in the shipbuilding and car industries and the TUC called a special congress in June 1969, for the first time in 40 years. Since becoming Party Treasurer Callaghan had developed close relationships with many trade union leaders and these now came into play as the Home Secretary led the fight in the Cabinet to stop the White Paper becoming law.

His relationship with Wilson became fraught particularly when Callaghan, attending Labour's National Executive on 26 March, voted for a motion rejecting *In Place of Strife* thus publicly breaching the convention of collective responsibility. Three other ministers, Eirene White, Alice Bacon and Fred Mulley, also voted against government policy. On 6 May the split in the party grew wider when Douglas Houghton, Chairman of the Parliamentary Labour Party warned the government against splitting with the TUC. Houghton was closely identified with Callaghan and the pair consulted each other on how best to oppose the proposals. He informed Houghton that if the Cabinet pushed through the penalty clauses, he would have to resign. A number of MPs began to talk of a leadership contest and Callaghan's name was mentioned as a possible contender. He was approached by several MPs to determine whether or not he would be willing to stand against Wilson. Callaghan rejected these approaches but the Prime Minister was aware of the unrest. Callaghan denied that he was motivated by presenting himself as a potential candidate for the leadership.

At the Cabinet meeting on 8 May both sides faced up to each other in an extremely tense meeting which removed any pretence of mutual respect. Crossman in his diaries relates what happened at this acrimonious meeting. In a discussion on Houghton's statement that the Parliamentary Party would not support the government when it came to a vote on the Industrial Relations Bill, Crossman raised the question of moves to remove the Prime Minister and said 'We have to sink or swim together' to which, according to Crossman, Callaghan interjected *Not sink or swim, sink or sink*, to which Crossman responded 'Why can't you resign if you think like that? Get out Jim, get out.'[4] Callaghan replied that if his colleagues wished him to resign from the Cabinet he would do so. This offer was not taken up by Cabinet members but within days Callaghan was to receive a major blow to his prestige within the government when Wilson called him to a meeting and informed him that although he did not wish him to resign as Home Secretary, several of his colleagues believed he should no longer be a member of the Inner Cabinet. In his memoirs Callaghan speculated that the colleagues concerned were Crossman and Castle.

On 12 May Wilson and Castle met the TUC when the first signs that an agreement could be reached which would avoid the government pressing ahead with its threat of legal sanctions were seen. Led by its General Secretary Vic Feather, the TUC tabled proposals to deal with inter-union disputes which would give the General Council the power to intervene in demarcation disputes and make a binding decision. Following the meeting Barbara Castle told the Inner Cabinet that the TUC had moved further and faster in the previous two weeks than they had in the past 40 years. There then followed a frantic series of meetings between the two sides before the TUC special congress in Croydon on 5 June which had been called to discuss the proposed legislation. At these meetings Wilson and Castle pressed the TUC to go further on their offer to police unofficial strikes but no agreement was reached.

Following the Congress, which predictably voted almost unanimously to oppose the legislation, the talks recommenced on 9 June. Unlike the TUC, Wilson and Castle did not have the luxury of knowing that their troops were fully behind them. They were not convinced that if the talks with the TUC broke down their Cabinet colleagues would back them and vote to press ahead with the legislation with the legal sanctions still included. Opposition to the proposed Bill was growing within the Cabinet, and although Ministers were content to allow the talks to continue there was a lack of enthusiasm for the contentious clauses.

This meant that Wilson had to play a game of poker with tough street-wise union bosses such as Jack Jones, head of the Transport and General Workers Union, and Hugh Scanlon of the Amalgamated Engineering Union, with few aces in his hand. Nevertheless, Wilson and Castle stuck to their task threatening the TUC leaders that failing an agreement the government would press ahead anyway. At a meeting at Number 10 on 18 June the TUC indicated their willingness to deal with unofficial strikes but still refused to countenance a rule change. To break the deadlock Wilson and Castle with the help of the Attorney General drafted a binding undertaking which they presented to the TUC for their consideration. The meeting adjourned to allow the TUC representatives time to consider the proposal. Meanwhile the Cabinet were waiting below in the Cabinet Room to hear the outcome. Finally at 5 p.m. Vic Feather informed Wilson that his colleagues had unanimously accepted the binding undertaking and were willing to sign it. The Cabinet were then informed that an agreement had been reached which allowed the government to withdraw penal sanctions from the Bill. The Cabinet agreed to the deal reached with the unions and the crisis was over. Callaghan however had damaged himself in many of his Cabinet colleagues' eyes by refusing to accept Cabinet collective responsibility. But Callaghan defended his actions saying: *I have taken this line from the beginning because I believe it to be right and in the best interests of the Party. I have never thought that the penalty clauses would ruin the unions and have consistently said that 90 per cent of the White Paper is not only acceptable but welcome ...*[5] In later years, however, Callaghan was to criticise the TUC for not delivering on their undertakings and for their failure to take action to curb unofficial strikes. In his memoirs he wrote: *In 1969 they still had the opportunity to demonstrate that autonomous self-governing institutions could respond to adverse public opinion and reform themselves. They failed to do so, and this coupled with the excesses of some activists in the 1970s, led inexorably to the Parliamentary legislation and the intervention by the courts in their affairs, a development I had always resisted.*[6]

Although Callaghan was unpopular with the Prime Minister and some Cabinet colleagues, including Denis Healey, his opposition to *In Place of Strife* was popular with many in the Parliamentary Labour Party. However, his opposition resulted in him being removed from the Inner Cabinet but his standing in the Cabinet was to be fully restored by his handling of the next impending crisis – Northern Ireland. Once again events were to play a key role in Callaghan's political career.

Northern Ireland, for all practical political purposes, had ceased to exist as far as the British government was concerned from the moment that the Government of Ireland Act was passed in 1920 and Ireland was partitioned. Pontius Pilate could not have done it better when it came to the washing of hands regarding any discrimination or acts of violence carried out by the Protestant majority against the Catholic minority. Since 1922 the Speaker of the House of Commons had ruled that Northern Ireland matters could not be raised in the Commons. This explains why during the 1960s the Commons spent less than two hours a year discussing Ulster. Callaghan, as Home Secretary, was willing to go along with this blind-eye approach until events in August 1969 forced him to act to prevent the slaughter of Catholics.

The root of the Northern Ireland problem can be traced back to its very inception when an artificial state was formed to allow Ulster Protestants to remain part of the United Kingdom. To ensure a viable state three counties with Catholic majorities were included within its borders, a fact ignored by the Boundary Commission in 1925. The Catholic minority had voted for Ireland to be independent of Britain in a nationwide poll but were forced into a Northern Irish state where they would be doomed to be a permanent minority, a fact reinforced by the legislation which gave the vote in elections to the Northern Ireland Parliament only to ratepayers. The Ulster Unionists who governed the Province from its foundation then proceeded to gerrymander the votes by not building houses for Catholics, and any houses which were built were crammed into existing wards to ensure that they did not lead to any additional representation for the Catholic minority. There was also wholesale job discrimination against Catholics. In his book *The Troubles* Tim Pat Coogan described how, in Derry City, where the population in 1961 was 53,744 of whom 36,049 were Catholic and the remaining 17,695 were Protestant, Londonderry Corporation employed 177 men – 145 who were Protestant and only 32 Catholic. In Harland & Wolff shipyard less than one in ten of the 5,000-plus workforce in the late 1960s were Catholic.

Discrimination such as this inevitably meant that a much larger proportion of the Catholic Nationalist population were unemployed.

It was conditions such as these which led to the formation of the Citizens Action Committee in October 1968. Sectarian violence had already broken out in Northern Ireland in 1966 – violence which was to last for more than 30 years and was to become known as 'The Troubles'. In May 1966 in response to claims by Ian Paisley that the Prime Minister of Northern Ireland Captain Terence O'Neil was selling-out Ulster, the Ulster Volunteer Force was re-formed and the first casualty came when the UVF petrol bombed a Catholic pub, killing a Protestant woman who lived next door. Several Catholics were to be murdered by the new Loyalist paramilitaries before the year was out yet the British government did not intervene directly, preferring to exert pressure on the Stormont government but remaining one step removed from the problem.

Twenty years later, according to Tim Pat Coogan, Callaghan, speaking at a seminar in London run by the Institute of Contemporary British History was much franker than usual. The question under discussion was: 'Did the Government miss an opportunity to take policy initiatives that could have prevented the breakdown of law and order in August 1969?' Addressing an audience which included several former British and Irish prime ministers, generals and senior civil servants Callaghan said: ... *the government very sensibly said we are not going to get involved in this when we are not welcomed by the Northern Ireland government. We would have to override the Northern Ireland government if we did. We're not going to do that. We want to use them as far as far as we can – that is what I understood the position was – in order to introduce the reforms ... everybody knew what would happen if we did intervene and nobody wanted to get into the situation that if we once got in there we would*

never get out. That was certainly my policy when I got there, which wasn't until '67, to use O'Neil to put the reforms through and not in any circumstances to get our fingers burned as indeed we have done when we eventually had to go in. And if we had gone in earlier we would have just got our fingers burned two years earlier that's all.[7]
The reason for Callaghan's frankness was that the seminar was being held under Chatham House rules which were aimed to guarantee confidentiality.

The policy described by Callaghan was in place before he became Home Secretary in December 1967. This is illustrated by the fact that although the sectarian killings had started some 18 months earlier there was no mention of Northern Ireland in the papers put before him when he took over responsibility for the Home Office. Callaghan finally intervened directly in August 1969 when rioting broke out in Derry and Belfast on a much greater scale than before. Shortland armoured personnel carriers armed with machine guns were deployed in Belfast, resulting in a nine-year-old boy, Patrick Rooney, being shot as he lay asleep in his bed. The Irish government established field hospitals at the border to deal with the wounded and thousands of Catholics fled to the Republic. Tension was heightened when the Irish Prime Minister Jack Lynch appeared on television to say that his government could not stand idly by and called for the UN to intervene.

Callaghan and Wilson were both on holiday, the Prime Minister in the Scillies, his favourite haunt, and Callaghan in Cornwall. They met in Culdrose, near Penzance on 14 August to discuss the worsening situation and agreed that if requested by the Stormont government they would commit troops but would demand a number of reforms in return. Events moved swiftly. In Stormont the Unionist deputy home affairs minister John Taylor announced that he was mobilising

11,000 B-Specials, a Protestant paramilitary force which the Nationalist Catholic population had good reason to fear.

But before the day was out the situation took a dramatic turn when the Minister for Home Affairs Robert Porter announced that Stormont had asked the British government to send in the army. The appeal was made under the guise that the RUC had information that the IRA was preparing to send armed units into Northern Ireland. It has been well-documented in the many studies of The Troubles that the IRA was in no position to mount any credible armed attacks. The Official IRA was not prepared for the events taking place in the North and had few weapons available to them. It is difficult to believe that the RUC were not aware of this fact but the British government, having received the request, agreed to it and the Cabinet at a meeting on 19 August ratified the decision to deploy troops in Northern Ireland. In his papers Crossman quoted Callaghan as saying to him over dinner: ... *it is enjoyable being Minister. It's much more fun being Home Secretary than the Chancellor. This is what I like doing, taking decisions, and I had to take the decision to put the troops in while I was in the plane on the way back from Cornwall.*[8] This was how it came about that members of The Prince of Wales Own Yorkshire Regiment under the command of General Freeland marched over Craigavon Bridge to take up positions in Derry.

It's much more fun being Home Secretary than the Chancellor.

CALLAGHAN

The soldiers were at first welcomed by the Nationalist communities in Belfast and Derry but this honeymoon period did not last, and before very long the British army found itself being treated as the enemy by both the Loyalists and the Republicans. At a meeting at Number 10 Wilson and Callaghan had demanded a raft of reforms from Major James Chichester-Clarke who had taken over from Captain

O'Neil as the Northern Ireland Prime Minister. Following the meeting a statement was issued which came to be known as the Downing Street Declaration listing a series of changes in the governance of Northern Ireland.

The British army took over responsibility for law and order and Sir John Hunt was appointed to head an inquiry into the RUC while the discredited B-Specials were to be phased out. Reforms were also promised in local government boundaries, the voting franchise and the allocation of housing. The statement also made clear that every citizen would be treated equally no matter their politics or religion.

Harold Wilson in his diaries made this comment: 'Had a previous United Kingdom government thought of drafting it, and insisted on its acceptance; more, had its non-discriminatory terms been accepted a generation, or even ten years, earlier the tragedy of August 1969 could have been averted, and Northern Ireland set peacefully on a new course. In this, as in so many other issues, the Labour government had to act at the eleventh hour, after years of neglect.'[9] True, but rather disingenuous. It ignores the fact that Labour was in power from 1964 and no attempt was made to tackle the blatant discrimination against Catholics in the five years up to 1969. Sectarian murders had been taking place since 1966 and nothing was done to radically alter the discriminatory policies of the Unionists or reform the police force. Callaghan's statement to the seminar in the 1980s quoted earlier in this chapter has more of a ring of truth about it. The Wilson government did not want to intervene in Northern Ireland and only did so when forced to. In this they were no different from any other British government dating back to the partition of Ireland.

The British media welcomed the Downing Street Declaration and carried stories describing how popular the British troops were with the Catholic population. Callaghan came in for a great deal of praise for taking decisive action. On 29 August he visited Northern Ireland, which Wilson described as a 'courageous' act and praised his Home Secretary for the manner in which he handled the situation. During his visit he went to the Bogside where the barricades had temporarily been removed and two white lines painted on the road in their place with the Army agreeing not to step over the lines. Callaghan however did and was immediately engulfed by an enthusiastic crowd who had been heartened by his words that the British government was not impartial but on the side of justice. During this visit the Scarman inquiry was announced to look into the cause of the riots. Following Callaghan's visit the first of the so-called Peace Lines were built to replace the barricades and divide the two warring communities. These barricades were to become permanent features during the Troubles.

The pace of reform quickened under Callaghan's guidance. Following the Hunt Report on the RUC and the disbandment of the B-Specials, Callaghan appointed Sir Arthur Young, a former City of London Police Commissioner, to replace Anthony Peacock who resigned following publication of the report at the beginning of October. The B-Specials were to be replaced by a part-time regiment, the Ulster Defence Regiment, which was to be an integral part of the British army. However, the UDR was also to remain an almost exclusive Protestant unit during its entire lifetime. A new Minister for Community Relations, Dr Robert Simpson, was appointed on 29 October, and on 24 November 1969 the Electoral Law Act (NI) introduced one man, one vote in local government elections in Northern Ireland. However, in January 1970 the honeymoon period the government had enjoyed since the troops were first deployed in August came to an end. The Provisional IRA emerged and what was to be called 'The Long War' was about to begin.

Wilson called a general election in June 1970 and to most commentators' surprise lost. Edward Heath became Prime Minister and Callaghan's tenure as Home Secretary was over. No one can deny that once galvanised into action Callaghan introduced much-needed reforms in Northern Ireland, which should not have taken more than 60 years to introduce. Callaghan, however, on his own admission went along with the British policy of non-intervention. His astute handling of Northern Ireland restored his relationship with Wilson and in the autumn of 1969 he had been restored to the Inner Cabinet. His standing in the country had risen and the *Guardian* newspaper named him 'Politician of the Year'. Following the general election defeat, Callaghan visited Northern Ireland in March 1971 to address a meeting in Ulster Hall at which he called for an All-Ireland Council to be discussed with the Irish Premier Jack Lynch. Heath rejected this suggestion but two years later it re-appeared in the Sunningdale Agreement.

It was not only Callaghan's personal political standing which showed improvement as the country moved into a new decade. The balance of payments for 1969 revealed a surplus of £286 million, allowing Britain to pay off its debts to the IMF. This allowed the Wilson government to reduce the bank rate to 7.5 per cent in March and in April Roy Jenkins announced a further cut to 7 per cent. Labour could be forgiven for feeling confident of a 1970 election victory boosted by a good performance in the district and borough elections in England and Wales which saw them gaining 447 seats. The Inner Cabinet agreed at their meeting on 12 May to Wilson's proposal to call an election for 18 June and on 18 May after an audience with the Queen, Wilson announced the election.

The only fly in the ointment was the MCC's decision to invite the South African cricket team to tour Britain. Anti-apartheid activists immediately declared their intention to stage protests and attempted to disrupt the tour. Labour realised that if the protests were to become violent with confrontations between the demonstrators and police then the tour could quickly turn into a law and order issue during the election. Callaghan invited the MCC to meet him. He asked them to cancel the tour 'on the grounds of broad public policy' and followed this up with a written request. The following day the MCC Cricket Council met and decided 'with deep regret' to cancel the tour. The Conservatives condemned the Home Secretary's actions but Callaghan must have been quietly pleased, having averted what could have been a major distraction during the election. During the campaign the opinion polls gave Labour a healthy lead over the Conservatives up until the last few days. Three days before polling came a piece of bad news. There was an unexpected deficit of £31 million in the balance of payments figures for May which were partly blamed on the purchase of Jumbo Jets from abroad.

Heath overtook Labour in the polls and led as the campaign drew to a close and the unthinkable began to dawn on Labour. The Conservatives won 330 seats to Labour's 288. Callaghan held on to his own Cardiff South-East seat but with a majority of 5,455, half of his previous majority. At the age of 58 Callaghan was back on the opposition benches, albeit on the Front Bench, but he could contemplate being able to spend more time on his Upper Clayhill Farm in Sussex in which he had purchased a 50 per cent share three years previously.

He became Shadow Home Secretary but with his party in opposition it appeared that the opportunity to become Prime Minister had passed him by. In 1972 Callaghan went into

Bart's hospital for an operation on his prostate which led him to give up smoking and later alcohol.

Then in 1973, following an approach by the Conservative Chancellor Anthony Barber, he agreed to allow his name to go forward for the powerful position of Managing Director of the International Monetary Fund. His wife Audrey was not enamoured with this proposed career move, and Callaghan himself admitted that he was relieved when the French government vetoed the suggestion. But the fact that he had allowed his name to go forward was a clear indication that Callaghan himself did not see his political career progressing further. He was also unhappy at the developments within the Labour Party with extreme left-wing groups who on their own would not receive the support of the electorate joining the Party to use it as a vehicle for their policies. They were to become political parties within the Labour Party with the Militant Tendency by far the most prominent. Militant had its own newspaper and also a number of paid full-time organisers. Few, including Callaghan, foresaw the havoc their presence was to cause Labour. The Militants targeted constituencies they believed they could gain control and install their own MPs and supported the call for the reselection of MPs and a greater say for members in the drafting of the election manifesto. There can be little doubt that Callaghan was one of the individuals they had in their sights.

Heath negotiated Britain's entry into the EEC and the Commons, on 28 October voted by 366 votes to 244 to become members. The pro-market vote included 69 Labour MPs, an indication of the split over the issue within the Parliamentary Labour Party. Britain was committed to taking its place on 1 January 1973. The Labour Party had never been keen supporters of the EEC and in April 1972 they had adopted a policy that, on their return to power they would hold a referendum on whether or not Britain should remain a member. The adoption of this policy resulted in Roy Jenkins, an enthusiastic supporter of the EEC, resigning as Deputy Leader and Shadow Chancellor; Denis Healey became Shadow Chancellor and Callaghan Shadow Foreign Secretary. Callaghan further strengthened his position within the Party when at the start of 1973 he succeeded Tony Benn as Labour Party Chairman.

Callaghan was on the eurosceptic wing of the Party with a greater affinity for the emerging Commonwealth countries and also the United States. He was instrumental in formulating the party's policy regarding new terms Labour should seek in the re-negotiations.

Callaghan had shown an interest in foreign affairs ever since entering Parliament. He had already established relationships with a number of African Commonwealth leaders thanks to his period as Colonial and Commonwealth spokesman in the late 1950s and early 1960s. He also enlisted the services of Tom McNally, who since 1969 had worked in the International Section of the Labour Party. McNally was to become a long-term member of Callaghan's staff acting as his political adviser during his premiership. Callaghan did not waste any time in mastering his new department. In August 1972, he visited Moscow to meet Shitikov, President of the Supreme Soviet, to discuss European security. At the start of 1973 he visited North and South Vietnam and neighbouring Laos during a ceasefire, meeting South Vietnam's President, Thieu and the Premier of North Vietnam Pham Van Dong. The following July he made a tour of Eastern Europe taking in Hungary, Bulgaria and Romania

The Heath government began to run into major difficulties following the oil embargo imposed by OPEC in 1973 on countries they considered had supported Israel in the Six Day

War resulting in the quadrupling of oil prices. The massive hike in oil prices saw Britain's trade deficit soar to £270 million in November and the bank rate rose to 13 per cent in January 1974. From January a three-day was imposed and offices were not allowed to use electricity at weekends. The National Union of Mineworkers (NUM) held a strike ballot and 81 per cent voted in favour of all-out industrial action to begin on 10 February. This prompted Heath to call a general election on 6 February asking the electorate to decide 'Who Governs Britain'.

Callaghan had been out of the country visiting the Middle East as the crisis developed. A general election had been expected at some point in 1974 and Callaghan wanted to ensure that the Arab countries would not impose an oil embargo on Britain if Labour was elected. This fear arose from the fact that the Labour Party had traditionally closer links with Israel than with the Arab countries. He met President Sadat of Egypt before travelling to Israel to meet Golda Meir, the Israeli Prime Minister. He took with him a message from President Sadat to say that Egypt desired peace with Israel. During the visit he received messages from Britain that a general election was imminent. When he stepped from the plane at Heathrow, he was met by a BBC reporter who informed him that Heath had called a general election only five minutes earlier. The NUM suspended their strike for the duration of the general election campaign and Callaghan was the main figure in the Labour Party's first ever television political broadcast.

Labour won 301 seats to the Conservative's 297 but the other parties held 37 seats between them. Callaghan held his own seat with a majority of 7,146, a slight improvement on his previous result. The Liberals had 14 seats and Heath, determined to hold on to power, opened negotiations with the

Liberal leader Jeremy Thorpe but grassroots Liberal opinion made it impossible for Thorpe to come to any agreement. The Ulster Unionists held 11 seats but were committed to destroying the Sunningdale Agreement which Heath was totally committed to, therefore ruling them out as possible partners in government. Heath had to accept that he could not form a government and resigned, leaving the way open for Wilson to form a minority Labour government.

Chapter 5: Foreign Secretary

A new Labour government took office in March 1974 but it contained many familiar figures who had been ministers in previous administrations. In addition to Wilson and Callaghan there were Healey as Chancellor of Exchequer and Jenkins who had wanted the Foreign Office but had to accept the Home Office. Others included Tony Benn at Trade and Industry and Barbara Castle in charge of Social Services. There was some new faces: Shirley Williams entered the Cabinet for the first time, as did Michael Foot at the age of 61 as Secretary for Employment, while Merlyn Rees, a Callaghan ally, became Secretary of State for Northern Ireland.

Callaghan retained his Foreign Office portfolio and was immediately faced with re-negotiating Britain's membership terms of the EEC which Labour while in office had committed themselves to doing. Callaghan was certainly not in the pro-European camp. He was determined to negotiate a major overhaul and was not willing to give any undertakings that Britain would remain in the Community which had now grown to eight with Denmark and Britain joining the original six. He was aware that the Labour Party and the Cabinet was divided into pro- and anti-market factions and realised that one of his priorities was to keep the government and party united, not an easy task.

Britain had four areas which it wished to renegotiate – the

Community Budget, the Common Agricultural Policy (CAP), access for Commonwealth products, and no interference in Britain's regional development policies. The formal negotiations began on 1 April 1974 in Luxembourg when Callaghan attacked the proposal for a European monetary union and the concept of a political European Union by 1980. At the same time he lambasted the CAP for its high costs while drawing attention to the amount Britain was expected to pay into the EC budget. His speech was not welcomed by the other EC leaders. The following month Callaghan met François Ortoli, chairman of the European Commission who indicated that there could be movement on some of Britain's grievances. This opened up the possibility of real negotiations, a process Callaghan understood from his trade union days.

Callaghan's approach to political problems was not driven by any ideology. He approached the negotiations in the way a trade union leader would approach an industrial problem. He looked for the best deal he could get and realised that this would require compromise. His lambasting of European leaders was his opening gambit: playing the rabid anti-market card so that his opponents later saw more progress than there really was. Callaghan knew he had to take the Cabinet and the Parliamentary Labour Party with him. He also knew that a general election would have to be called in the near future as the minority Labour government was suffering defeats in the Commons. The other European leaders were well aware of the political realities in Britain and at a Heads of Government meeting on 14 September in Paris it was agreed that there would be a further meeting in December to discuss the matter. This was made in the knowledge that Britain's second general election of 1974 would have taken place by then.

Meanwhile the enmity between the ethnic communities on the island of Cyprus rapidly descended into armed conflict, throwing together some strange partnerships and dividing previous allies. During the 1960s Britain had exiled Archbishop Makarios to the Seychelles for his support of 'Enosis' (union with Greece) but when Cyprus became independent in 1960 under a constitution backed by a Treaty of Guarantee signed by Britain, Greece and Turkey Makarios became President. Having tasted independence, he cooled on the concept of Enosis. This did not endear him to the Greek military government while as leader of a Commonwealth country his relations with Britain improved. Makarios finally demanded on 2 July that Greece withdraw its troops from the island, which resulted in the Greek National Guard stationed in Cyprus occupying the Presidential palace and overthrowing Makarios. Nicos Sampson, a former member of EOKA, the Greek Cypriot guerrilla force, was installed as President. Britain intervened on the diplomatic level as a signatory of the Treaty of Guarantee.

Turkey reacted immediately by announcing that it no longer considered Greece to be a guarantor of the Treaty and called on Britain to assist a Turkish invasion of the island to protect the Turkish Cypriot minority. Britain's response was to urge both sides to refrain from military action and declared it would not recognise Nicos Sampson as President. At the same time Callaghan approached Henry Kissinger, the US Secretary of State, to ask the US to put pressure on the Greek junta. Kissinger in his memoirs had this to say of working with Callaghan: 'We had every reason to welcome Callaghan's participation. There was no foreign leader with whom I enjoyed working more and very few I appreciated as much. Combining an avuncular personality with abundant good sense, Callaghan had rescued Anglo-American ties from the coolness into which Prime Minister Edward (Ted) Heath had plunged them in his attempt to demonstrate his commitment to Europe by dissociating, at least to some extent, from the "special relationship" with the United States.'[1]

The situation rapidly deteriorated, with Greece threatening to impose unity with Greece and the Turks bombing Greek Cypriot positions as Greece assembled a fleet of warships. The USA was reluctant to intervene and resisted British attempts to take the issue to the UN. The crisis deepened when on 20 July Turkish forces landed on Cyprus. Callaghan called on the Greek and Turkish governments to attend a tripartite meeting with Britain as signators of the Treaty of Guarantee. At the same time Britain moved troops into positions alongside UN forces to prevent any further advance by Turkish troops on Nicosia airport. The US also began to exert pressure on both countries and on 22 July a ceasefire was declared. The following day the Greek junta collapsed.

The tripartite talks finally got underway and an interim agreement was reached on 30 July in which the two adversaries agreed to make the ceasefire permanent while a buffer zone patrolled by UN forces would be created. The talks continued into August but broke up without a conclusive agreement and the island remains partitioned at the time of writing. President Nixon resigned on 8 August. If the US had acted earlier to put pressure on both countries would this have stopped the crisis escalating and the Mediterranean island being partitioned? Kissinger recognised the different approach the two countries had to the crisis but put this down to Callaghan's lack of experience in foreign affairs: 'The drawback of Callaghan's leading role was that it was his first exposure to crisis diplomacy, and Cyprus was about as intractable and maddening a problem as could be wished on any diplomat.'[2]

Wilson called the expected election, the second in six months, for 10 October. The result was not a great improvement for Labour, who with 319 seats to the Conservatives' 277 still only had an overall majority of three when the other parties were taken into account. Callaghan himself held on to Cardiff South-East, easily improving his majority over the Conservative candidate to 10,718. The pace now quickened in the EC negotiations as Callaghan improved his relations with both the French and the Germans. Helmut Schmidt, the West German Chancellor, was invited to address the delayed Labour Party Conference on 30 November during which he secured from Wilson and Callaghan the agreement that if the conclusion on the EC budget contributions were satis-factory to them they would make a positive recommenda-tion to Parliament that Labour should stay in. There were also positive meetings with the new French President Valery Giscard d'Estaing on 19 November and 5 December at the Elysée Palace to be followed on 9 December the Heads of Government summit Paris. Callaghan wrote in his memoirs: ... *I could feel the tide flowing in our direction* ... [3] Agreement was reached on the sugar quota which was of vital importance to West Indies producers and it was agreed that a European Regional Fund would be established to assist areas experienc-ing industrial decline.

While Wilson and Callaghan could see greater unity developing among the European counterparts they still faced a divided Cabinet at home. Wilson, addressing a meeting of Labour mayors, revealed for the first time in public that if the terms were right he would be recommending that Britain remained in the Community. The next summit meeting was arranged to be held in Dublin in March 1975 and Wilson and Callaghan hoped that they would be able to conclude the negotiations. This proved to be the case; concessions were made in relation to New Zealand dairy products. The final breakthrough came when the Summit agreed that any country

Helmut Schmidt

'The NATO decision to deploy intermediate-range missiles (of 1,500-mile range) in Europe dated from the Carter Administration. Its purpose was to assuage West German Chancellor Helmut Schmidt's outrage at the unilateral American cancellation of the so-called neutron bomb – designed to make nuclear war less destructive – which Schmidt had supported over the opposition of his own Social Democratic Party. The intermediate-range weapons (partly ballistic missiles, partly ground-launched cruise missiles) were in fact designed for a different problem – to counter the large number of new Soviet missiles (the SS-20s) that were capable of reaching all European targets from deep within Soviet territory. In its essence, the argument in favour of the intermediate-range weapons was political, not strategic, and it stemmed from the same concerns which twenty years earlier had generated allied debates about strategy; this time, however, America tried to allay Europe's fears. Bluntly put, once again the issue was whether Western Europe could count on the United States' using its nuclear weapons to repel a Soviet attack that was confined to Europe. Had America's European allies truly believed in America's willingness to resort to nuclear retaliation from the continental United States or from weapons based at sea, the new missiles on European soil would have been unnecessary. But America's resolve to do that was precisely what European leaders continued to doubt. For their part, American leaders had their own reasons for responding to European anxieties. It was part of the flexible response strategy to bring about opinions between all-out war focused on America and acceding to Soviet nuclear blackmail. There was, of course, a more sophisticated explanation than a subliminal mutual distrust between the two sides of the Atlantic partnership. And that was that the new weapons organically linked the strategic defense of Europe with that of the United States.... Thus the intermediate-range missiles closed a gap in the spectrum of deterrence ... the Soviet Union would not be able to attack either area without incurring an unacceptable risk of a general nuclear war.' [Henry Kissinger, *Diplomacy* (Simon & Schuster, New York: 1994) pp 775f.]

which found that it was contributing more to the overall budget than the appropriate percentage of its Gross Domestic Product would be entitled to a rebate. The maximum refund was set at around £125 million a year. Wilson and Callaghan left the meeting at this point to discuss their position and both agreed that they could accept this formula while retaining the right to return to the subject if the results did not turn out as they expected.

At the following press conference in Dublin Castle, Callaghan told the world's media that he would recommend to the Cabinet that Britain should accept the new terms. The eurosceptic had completed his conversion. Callaghan, while remaining a firm believer in Britain's special relationship with the US, also believed that Britain required to be in Europe. The package was put to the Cabinet in London at a two-day meeting, 17/18 March, and was endorsed by 16 votes to 7. It was also agreed that Cabinet members could campaign for the 'No' side in the inevitable campaign in the lead-up to the Referendum but could not campaign within Labour's National Executive against the government.

The matter went to Parliament, where Callaghan emphasised that Commonwealth countries were in favour of British acceptance. Although Parliament voted by a large majority to accept the terms, a number of Labour MPs voted to reject and a specially-convened Labour Party conference voted overwhelmingly to reject the package despite pleas from the Prime Minister and Callaghan. It was this chasm of opinion within the Labour movement that Callaghan had to deal with during the talks. They had to avoid the Party becoming engulfed in Civil War. The fact that he succeeded indicates a high degree of leadership using the skills he had honed in the trade union movement. For although the credit must be shared with Wilson as Prime Minister, it was Callaghan who was involved in the nitty-gritty of negotiations and who had been given by Wilson himself a free hand in handling the talks. The referendum on 5 June 1975 resulted in a decisive vote in favour of the package with 17.3 million voting in favour and 8.4 million against. Britain's future was now tied to Europe, although the same budgetary arguments have continued as have political and monetary union.

There were many other weighty matters on Callaghan's desk during his period as Foreign Secretary including European security. The Cold War was showing signs of thawing but there was still a definite chill in relationships between East and West. Callaghan believed that the arms race was beginning to take its toll on the Soviet economy. A Conference on Security and Cooperation in Europe (CSCE) was due to be held in Helsinki on 1 August. Callaghan attended the CSCE meeting which reached significant decisions including the recognition of post-war borders, a *de facto* recognition of the Soviet Union which had several previously independent countries within its borders. The conference also agreed that there should be greater protection for human rights. During 1975 he also visited Uganda where President Idi Amin's government had sentenced a British lecturer, Dennis Hills to death in April for writing an unpublished book critical of Amin. The visit was part of an agreement to secure the release of Hills who was duly freed in Callaghan's presence.

The Falklands also became an issue during Callaghan's tenure at the Foreign Office in 1975. Callaghan had met the Argentine Foreign Minister in New York in September 1974 following which he met their ambassador to the UK when he made it clear the desire of the island's population was to remain British but suggested the possibility of economic co-operation with Argentine in the field of oil exploration in the seas around the islands. However, Argentina continued to make territorial claims on the islands. Callaghan stressed to Wilson that Britain must leave Argentina in no doubt that they would act to defend the sovereignty of the Falklands. To this end after discussions with the Defence Secretary Roy Mason it was agreed that the Antarctic patrol vessel HMS *Endurance* should be sent to the South Atlantic to be stationed at Port Stanley where it remained until Margaret Thatcher's government withdrew it in 1982, a decision which Callaghan criticised in the Commons at the time. Once again Callaghan displayed political finesse. The issue did not attract much comment in 1975 but if Callaghan had not sent the correct signals to Argentina then the Falklands War could have taken place seven years earlier. The great irony is that Mrs Thatcher won a general election on the back of patriotic fervour for a war caused by political miscalculation while Callaghan received few plaudits for ensuring that a conflict did not take place.

As 1975 drew to a close Callaghan set off on a tour of Southern Africa to consult with Commonwealth members in the region on the question of Rhodesia. His visit took in Botswana, Kenya, Malawi, Nigeria, South Africa and Zambia. Among others he met President Vorster of South Africa but Ian Smith refused to allow an ANC delegation to leave the country to meet him. The tour did not change his view that there was no longer a quick fix as far as Rhodesia was concerned and that the problem would be around for some time.

Callaghan was now recognised as a leading figure on the world stage. He was in some people's eyes already an elder statesman having held the three main offices of state in Britain, Chancellor, Home Secretary and now Foreign Secretary. He was 63 and had admitted to colleagues that he no longer felt a great urge to be Prime Minister. Harold Wilson was younger than him, and when he moved aside Callaghan fully expected a younger member of the Cabinet to be elected leader of the party and if Labour was still in power to become Prime Minister, but once again events were to intervene.

Part Two

THE LEADERSHIP

Chapter 6: Prime Minister

Most of the Cabinet may have been shocked by Harold Wilson's announcement on 16 March 1976 that he intended to resign as Prime Minister but Callaghan was not. He had been alerted some weeks previously by a Cabinet colleague that the Prime Minister's resignation was in the offing. Wilson himself informed Callaghan of his intention to resign five days previously at a party given to mark his 60th birthday. Callaghan, who was only a few days away from his 64th birthday on 27 March, immediately put his name forward for the highest political position in the land. Two others, Michael Foot and Roy Jenkins, followed suit. Within days they had been joined by Denis Healey and Tony Crosland with Tony Benn being the last Cabinet member to enter the fray.

It was the first time the Labour Party had selected its leader while in office. The electorate was confined to MPs and the voting system was done by exhaustive ballot. Both wings of the party were reflected among the candidates with Tony Benn furthest to the left and Roy Jenkins furthest right. Michael Foot represented many left-wing MPs while Healey, Crosland and Callaghan could all be described as centre-right. Callaghan's election team was run by Merlyn Rees, a long-time ally, and Gregor Mackenzie both of whom had served as Parliamentary Private Secretaries to Callaghan. The election took place on 25 March and there was no surprise when

Michael Foot won the first ballot attracting 100 votes. It was also easy to calculate the total size of the left-wing vote with Tony Benn gaining 37 votes. Callaghan came second with 84 votes, followed by Jenkins, 56, Healey 30 and Crosland 17 votes. Jenkins, Benn and Crosland all withdrew and in the second ballot Callaghan came first with 141 votes, Foot second with 133 votes and Healey last with 38 votes. In the third and final ballot Callaghan won the leadership contest with 176 votes to Foot's 137.

The heavyweight *Financial Times* had supported Healey in the leadership contest but not surprisingly this was not a journal that most Labour MPs consulted for political guidance. This was the result which most pundits had expected. Only 12 months previously Callaghan's stature had been enhanced by his handling of the European Community renegotiations and he was by far the most experienced politician in the field having been Chancellor, Home Secretary and Foreign Secretary. The son of a Petty Officer who had to rely on the Ministry of Pensions to pay his school fees and who left school at 17 to enter the Civil Service at the lowest level was now Prime Minister. He is reputed to have said, when hearing the result of the election, *And I never went to university*. Callaghan felt some resentment that, unlike most of his colleagues, he had not had a university education.

And I never went to university.

CALLAGHAN

Callaghan's first job was to put his Cabinet together and put his mark on how his government would differ from that of his predecessor. Some positions such as Chancellor provided no surprises. Denis Healey had proved to be competent and retained his position. A replacement for Callaghan at the Foreign Office was not so simple, however. Jenkins wanted the position but having resigned over Labour's decision to seek re-negotiation of Britain's entry terms to the EC Jenkins would provide an easy target for the sizeable number of MPs who were still emotionally anti-European Community. Callaghan opted for Tony Crosland, prompting Jenkins to approach him requesting that the Prime Minister nominate him for the position of President of the European Commission. Callaghan granted his request. Jenkins remained as Home Secretary until he was appointed President of the European Commission five months later and was succeeded by Merlyn Rees at the Home Office. Michael Foot was also granted his request when he asked Callaghan if he could be appointed Leader of the House. This was a crucial position, given Labour's position as a minority government. Despite their political differences Callaghan immediately agreed as he had nothing but respect for Foot both as a politician and as a person. Albert Booth, who had been Foot's deputy under Wilson at the Department of Employment, replaced Foot. There was no great surprise when Barbara Castle, whose relationship with Callaghan was bruised during the *In Place of Strife* episode, was not given a position in the Cabinet. David Ennals took over her responsibilities at Health. Overall Callaghan's new Cabinet was more inclined to the right than Wilson's which had been more balanced. On the day that Callaghan formally moved into Number 10 Downing Street, 5 April, the *Financial Times* had this advice regarding how the new Prime Minister should tackle the problems facing the country: 'To persuade his supporters that the sacrifices now demanded will bring their rewards, and that is only by meeting the challenge, rather than by retreating into still deeper debt behind protective barriers, that we can achieve sound growth and full employment.'[1] Unlike the authors of the *Financial Times* leader column, Callaghan already had experience at the coal face.

The Wilson government had taken steps to curb wage inflation which was running at almost 25 per cent a week. In July 1975 a voluntary agreement had been reached with the TUC that wage rises would be limited to £6 a week for all workers earning less than £8,000 a year. This resulted in a dramatic decrease in the level of wage increases and eventually in wage inflation being reduced to single figures by early 1978. Despite this progress Sterling remained under pressure and in November 1975 Healey had to negotiate additional special drawing rights with the IMF with the first tranche of $1,800 million being handed over in January 1976. These were the circumstances Healey was faced with on Callaghan's second day in office when he set out his Budget. Healey told the Commons that he was aiming for wage increases being limited to 3 per cent. This target was not one which the trade unions welcomed and after only a few weeks in office Callaghan met the TUC General Council and spelled out bluntly that if the government and TUC could not reach an agreement on wage restraint then the Labour government would not survive.

Healey and Foot held a series of tough negotiations with the TUC which resulted in a voluntary agreement for 1977/78 of a minimum wage increase of £2.50 per week or 5 per cent whichever was the higher, and a maximum increase of £4 per week. It is interesting that in his memoirs Callaghan described how Healey had told him 'We cannot expect a third year of very severe restraint, yet we cannot afford renewed wage inflation.'[2] Perhaps a prophetic statement! Callaghan praised the trade unions for accepting their responsibility to wider society and admitted that the voluntary wage agreement bought time for the Labour government to tackle the underlying problems in the economy. A specially-convened TUC in June voted overwhelmingly in favour of the renewed Social

Contract in which the government committed itself to act where possible on trade union concerns.

It is a tribute to Callaghan and Healey's powers of persuasion that the trade union leaders, whose jobs were to improve the standard of living of their members and who had to face up to members being told to accept wage rises less than 5 per cent with inflation running at a much higher figure, voted for the policy. The TUC General Council accepted the deal by 20 votes to 3 against while Labour's National Executive, whose members bore no direct responsibility in the field of wages voted first by 11 to 8 to refer the package back although at a later meeting they endorsed it but only after Congress had accepted it.

Throughout this period Sterling continued to be under pressure and on 7 June the government announced standby credit of $5.3 billion from the US Treasury and the central banks of Germany, Japan, Canada, France and Switzerland. This however was a short-term measure as the money had to be repaid in six months. Despite these economic problems Labour, within six weeks of Callaghan becoming Prime Minister, still managed to push through Parliament by 304 votes to 303 the nationalisation

The Social Contract was a unique concept which offered trade unions a government programme of reductions in tax and increases in benefits in return for restraint in wage claims. It was first introduced into the political arena by Harold Wilson and Vic Feather of the TUC as a joint policy document, *Economic Policy and the Cost of Living* in January 1973. The aim of the contract was to reduce wage inflation. One major government initiative seen as part of the Social Contract was the introduction of the Advisory and Conciliation Service (ACAS) in 1974 but there were also job creation schemes and temporary employment subsidies brought in by the Labour governments under Wilson and Callaghan.

of the shipbuilding and aircraft industries which came into force the following year.

The pound remained fairly stable until September when it began to plunge in value against the dollar. Denis Healey in his memoirs was to describe the remaining months of 1976 as 'the worst of my life'. Callaghan was frustrated by Britain's currency and balance of payments problems, particularly as the long-term solution was on the horizon. Oil had been discovered in the North Sea off the coast of Scotland and the country was soon to become an oil-producing state. This would allow Britain to offset its oil imports against oil exports, eventually becoming a net energy exporter. There was also the prospect of gas discoveries providing the prospect of massive savings in energy imports. The difficulty was that these benefits were in the future, although not too far in the future. BP's massive Forte Field had been discovered in 1974. Once again displaying his visionary talents, Callaghan suggested to Healey that he raise the question of replacing the short-term credit with a long-term loan so that the repayments would be due at a time when Britain was enjoying the benefits of being an oil producer. The Chancellor put forward the Prime Minister's suggestion in private meetings while attending with Callaghan the Industrial Seven meeting in Puerto Rico. There was a disappointing reaction to the idea and nothing came of it.

Inflation was running at 14 per cent and by the end of September the exchange rate of the pound against the dollar had plunged to $1.63 but was to fall further to $1.50 causing Healey and the Governor of the Bank of England Gordon Richardson to return to London from Heathrow Airport, cancelling their planned trip to the Commonwealth finance ministers meeting in Hong Kong. The financial markets were in turmoil and it was hastily announced that the government was seeking a massive $3.9 million loan from the IMF. The

Labour Party Conference was in session in Blackpool and after some dithering Callaghan agreed that his Chancellor should come north and address the conference on 30 September. This was to prove to be a mistake of almost unimaginable proportion. Television viewers around the world were to witness Britain's Chancellor of Exchequer being booed by members of his own political party. The gulf between the party membership and the government was there for everyone to see. Callaghan had already warned of the dangers of entryism those dangers were there for all to see. The extreme left wing activists whose traditions were not those of Labour felt no loyalty to the Parliamentary Labour Party or the members of a Labour government. They had their own agenda and every section of the Labour movement, including the trade unions was to suffer from the corroding and energy-sapping effects of their sectarian attacks which were to continue until Neil Kinnock expelled them from the Labour Party in 1986. Healey was humiliated that day. Here was the country's Chancellor, grappling with one of the country's most serious ever crises, being booed to and from the rostrum, and only being allowed to speak for five minutes – the time allotted to a delegate!

No doubt part of the reaction among some of the delegates was to the unpopular cuts in public expenditure which the government already had to make and the voluntary wage restraint being asked for, but perhaps some of the negative reaction came as a result of the speech which Callaghan had made earlier to conference

What is the cause of unemployment? Quite simply and unequivocally it is caused by paying ourselves more than the value of what we produce.

CALLAGHAN

when he told the delegates: *What is the cause of unemployment? Quite simply and unequivocally it is caused by paying ourselves more than the value of what we produce.* Bluntly, he went on to tell the delegates: *We used to think that you could spend your way out of recession and increase employment by cutting taxes and boosting Government spending. I tell you in all candour that that option no longer exists ...* [3] This message did not sit well with the delegates. It appeared to be a renunciation of the full-employment policy all governments since the Second World War had pursued.

Callaghan had taken great care over this particular speech and was personally responsible for its content. He was attempting to inject some reality into the way the Labour Party members and trade unionists viewed the economic problems facing the country. This speech has been interpreted in some quarters as being the first flickering of monetarism in post-war Britain putting the fight against inflation ahead of the aim of maintaining full employment. There is an argument for this but Callaghan was never a full-blown monetarist. In the looming negotiations with the IMF he set his face against their most extreme proposals which would have resulted in high unemployment. Indeed he tried to avoid having to go into further hock with the IMF. He believed Britain could look forward to a prosperous future in the medium term when North Sea oil began to flow. He also remained a firm believer in governing by consensus and not by diktat. Callaghan was certainly no free marketeer.

Callaghan was reluctant to accept the stringent cuts the IMF were expected to demand in return for a further loan. He was also against using import controls to tackle the problem. Immediately after the Labour Party Conference at the end of September he began to lobby President Gerald Ford and Helmut Schmidt of Germany to use their influence to moderate the IMF demands and to consider a possible long-term solution. However, President Ford had other things on his mind. He was facing a election in a few weeks time against

Jimmy Carter, an election he eventually lost. Schmidt, for all his good intentions, did not have the legal power to instruct the Bundesbank how to act in the financial markets and he was also facing Federal elections in December.

Meanwhile Healey was busy with his Treasury officials putting together the case they would make to the IMF team when they arrived the following month. Healey was of the view that an IMF loan was the only deal on the table. Callaghan, having experience of the Treasury in his time as Chancellor, did not fully agree with their approach to Sterling's problems and felt as Prime Minister he could use his influence with other leaders to find an alternative solution. This two-pronged strategy resulted in friction between Callaghan and Healey. The difference in approach was highlighted when Healey approached Callaghan on 6 October for his backing to raise the Minimum Lending Rate by 2 per cent to 15 per cent. Callaghan at first refused and it was not until the following day that he conceded. Callaghan was determined to hold out against swingeing cuts in public expenditure. In addition to behind-the-scenes manoeuvres he also went public on the BBC *Panorama* programme on 25 October: *I would love to get rid of the reserve currency. I am not sure that everybody in the Treasury would, maybe in the Bank. But from Britain's point of view I see no particular advantage in being a reserve currency at all.*[4] He also hinted that Britain might withdraw its troops from Germany. Callaghan was determined that the Public Sector Borrowing Requirement (PSBR) of £9 billion the Cabinet had agreed in July would not be reduced. He wanted to buy time. Inflation was heading towards single figures and was predicted to reach 8 per cent by 1978 if the social contract with the TUC held and wage constraints continued. Oil revenues were also beginning to flow. Meanwhile Sterling had come under renewed attack and sunk to a level of $1.53 on 28 October.

The IMF negotiating team arrived on 1 November but did not meet the Treasury negotiators until 10 November. Their opening gambit was to demand a breathtaking £3 billion of cuts in the PSBR for 1977–8 and a further £4 billion in 1978–9. Callaghan was still involving himself in the delicate negotiations. On 1 December he met Johannes Witteveen, managing director of the IMF, who had flown to London for a face-to-face early morning secret meeting. Healey was aware of the meeting but was not present; the only other British person in the room was Sir Kenneth Stowe, Callaghan's Principal Private Secretary. The IMF executive insisted on immediate public expenditure cuts with Callaghan trying to hold the line at £2 billion. After much haggling and threats of ending the meeting, Witteveen eventually proposed cuts of £2.5 billion over the two years 1977–9.

Britain's Chancellors often refer to the Public Sector Borrowing Requirement (PSBR) with much nodding of heads in the crowded Commons chamber but what is the PSBR? It is the deficit of central government, local authority and public corporations. It is financed by borrowing from the private sector at home and abroad or by increasing the domestic money supply. Governments have to keep the PSBR under control as the more the public services borrow in the financial markets, the higher interest rates become. The alternative of increasing money supply can push up inflation so this option is not favoured.

Callaghan then had the difficult job of persuading the Cabinet to accept the proposed cuts. There were a number of factions within the Cabinet supporting different methods of approaching the problem, and Callaghan was aware that Healey did not command a majority for his approach. Callaghan himself had been keeping his options open as he was determined to guide the Cabinet through this crisis and avoid a repeat of 1931 when Ramsey MacDonald's Labour government resigned in the middle of an economic crisis and MacDonald formed a National Government with the Conservative Party.

Tony Benn, backed by other Cabinet left-wingers, supported import controls while Peter Shore was also for a protectionist policy and Tony Crosland wanted to introduce a system of import deposits. On the first day of the Cabinet meeting Callaghan allowed each faction to expound their alternatives while keeping his own counsel. Healey took the floor the following day when he spelled out that Britain had few options. He told the Cabinet that he believed the IMF would accept smaller cuts than they had first demand. He proposed putting forward £1 billion of cuts for 1977–8 plus £500 million from the sale of BP shares. There would then be further cuts of £1.5 billion in 1978–9. Callaghan then revealed his support for the Chancellor's proposals. The Cabinet finally accepted these proposals which still left a gap between the government and the IMF. Healey met the IMF the following day when the IMF team put forward £1 billion in the first tranche of cuts and £3 billion in the second. There then followed a stand-off during which Healey threatened the IMF with Labour calling a general election. The IMF team blinked first and a settlement was reached. The Cabinet then met on 7 December and began to hammer out how the first £1 billion of savings would be made which they managed without repeating the social benefit cuts of 1931. On 15 December Healey announced the terms of the IMF's £3.9 million loan.

Callaghan could claim that his approach had been correct although it inevitably produced tensions between himself and his Chancellor. Subsequent events were to prove that he was correct in not trusting the Treasury's forecasts relating to the PSBR. The government's borrowing requirements for the 1977–9 period proved to be far less than the Treasury forecasts. Callaghan's efforts had at least reduced the cuts. His handling of the Cabinet also showed great skill. His stance on Sterling's position as a reserve currency also proved correct. On January 1977 Healey announced that Sterling balances would be run down with the help of a $1.5 billion loan from European banks. The result of this announcement was an inflow of $2 billion into Sterling and gilt-edged securities during January.

On 28 January the Minimum Lending Rate was reduced by 1 per cent to 12.5 per cent and 12 months later was to stand at 8.5 per cent. By spring Sterling was enjoying the positive effects of the government's actions with the pound's exchange rate with the dollar reaching $1.80 in April and the country's reserves almost doubled from $4 billion at end of April to $7.2 billion by the end of June. In his Budget in March 1977 Healey was able to announce £2.3 billion of tax cuts, yet another indication that Callaghan had been correct in his belief that the cuts initially demanded by the IMF were not justified. Britain's stance was further vindicated by the fact that Britain only needed to draw half of the IMF loan. The minority Labour government could be pleased with how they came through the crisis and Callaghan is due recognition for how he personally dealt with it.

Chapter 7: The Lib-Lab Pact

Callaghan had every reason to believe at the beginning of 1977 that the country had turned the corner as all the economic indicators were positive but there was still a major problem. His government was a minority in the Commons and unless he could find political allies Labour would be brought down and with the electorate yet to feel the practical benefits of the sacrifices they had had to make there was every possibility that a quick general election would see the Conservatives returned to power to enjoy the fruits of Labour's efforts. Callaghan deeply felt the loss of Tony Crosland who died on 19 February after suffering a stroke. He was replaced as Foreign Secretary by his young deputy David Owen who was only 38.

Callaghan did not have much time to find the votes he needed to keep Labour in power. The Conservative leader, Margaret Thatcher had given notice that the Opposition would move a vote of no confidence on 23 March. Callaghan had few choices open to him. The ten Ulster Unionist MPs were a motley crew and traditionally had sided with the Conservatives in the Commons. The Scottish Nationalist Party's 11 MPs were thought to be unlikely to vote against the government in a no confidence vote as they trusted Labour to deliver on devolution more than they did the Conservatives but they were unlikely to co-operate with Labour on the many issues the government required to get through

Parliament. There was also Plaid Cymru but their three MPs held widely differing political views, only agreeing on the need for a Welsh assembly.

The problem facing Labour was highlighted in February on a vote on the Devolution Bill when the government was defeated by 312 votes to 283 with 22 Labour MPs voting against it and another 15 abstaining. This was an indication of the difficulties Labour had on this issue. The party was divided even within Scotland and the political reality was that they were being forced down the devolution route by the success of the SNP. Scottish MPs such as Tam Dalyell, Bob Hughes and Norman Buchan had set their faces against devolution and were supported by a sizeable number of English MPs. One symptom of this divide had come in December 1975 when Jim Sillars MP left the Labour Party to form the Scottish Labour Party (SLP), followed by John Robertson, a Paisley MP. The SLP was only short-lived but it highlighted the divisions within Labour in Scotland. Callaghan himself was not an ardent devolutionist but had been persuaded of its political necessity. The departure from the Labour ranks of the two MPs transformed the Labour government into a minority government.

The government's need to find political allies in the Commons could not, and did not prevent Callaghan carrying out the many responsibilities that come with being Prime Minister, including overseas visits. Callaghan visited Washington to meet the newly installed President Carter on 10–12 March. They were quickly to establish a working relationship, helped by the fact that the American President, like Callaghan, had served in his country's navy and was brought up in the Baptist church.

On his return to London Callaghan found that little headway had been made in finding voting partners but their

The Carter Doctrine

'Events during the 1970s demonstrated vividly that the East-West and North-South conflicts cannot be divorced from each other; they interact … talk of U.S. military intervention in 1973–1974 to seize the Persian Gulf oil fields was usually met with concern about Soviet intervention. Indeed, the fear that the Soviet Union, a "northern" state, might seek to dominate the nearby "southern" oil states was strengthened by the Soviet invasion of Afghanistan and led to the Carter Doctrine.' [John Spanier, *American Foreign Policy Since World War II* (Holt, Rinehart and Winston, New York: 1983) p 298.] It is very clear that the United States considered British interests resulting from historical links to particular areas secondary to these global strategic considerations. Gone were the times when F D Roosevelt intimated that only if his suggestion met with "the cordial approval and whole-hearted support of His Majesty's Government" would he then approach the Governments of France, Germany and Italy on convening a conference to reduce international tensions about the Italian occupation of Abyssinia. President Carter, not knowing where the Soviets might strike next, proclaimed his Doctrine, telling the world that 'an attempt by any outside force to gain control of the Persian Gulf region will be regarded as an assault on the vital interests of the United States of America, and such an assault will be repelled by use of any means necessary, including military force.' He committed his allies to follow where America would lead. 'More important, Carter consented to the kinds of covert action he had never previously approved, travelling a path that soon led him to intervene in Angola, Ethiopia, Mozambique, and South Yemen, all quasi-Marxist states sustained by the Soviet Union. Admiral Stansfield Turner, head of the CIA, who had long pressed the President to be more aggressive, wrote: "This it was the at the Carter administration, despite its dedication to human rights and considerable reservations about the morality of covert actions, turned easily and quickly to covert devices."'[Stephen Graubard, *The Presidents* (Allen Lane, London: 2004) p 543.]

search for Commons votes were answered when Liberal Party leader David Steel, a Scottish Borders MP, wrote indicating that his party wished to be 'consulted on broad policy issues.' Callaghan told Michael Foot, Cledwyn Hughes, Chairman of the Parliamentary Labour Party, and the Labour whips to make contact with the Liberals, and on 21 March he met Steel. There then followed a flurry of meetings and the next day the Lib-Lab pact was born.

The government issued a joint statement with the Liberals describing the aims of the pact on 23 March: 'We agreed today the basis on which the Liberal Party would work with the Government in the pursuit of economic recovery. We will set up a joint consultative committee under the chairmanship of the Leader of the House which will meet regularly. The committee will examine government policy and other issues prior to their coming before the House, and Liberal policy proposals. The existence of this committee will not commit the Government to accepting the views of the Liberal Party or the Liberal Party to supporting the Government on any issue.'[1]

A joint consultative committee would be formed and there would be regular meetings between Chancellor Denis Healey and the Liberal economic spokesman John Pardoe. There would be direct elections to the European Assembly and MPs would be given a free vote to decide the type of voting system to be used in the election due in 1979. The Liberals, who traditionally were a strong devolutionist party, also received an undertaking that there would be an injection of momentum into Scottish and Welsh devolution which would be dealt with as two separate Bills to replace the unified original Bill. In return the Liberals promised to deliver their votes to ensure that the government would not fall in the House of Commons.

The Cabinet met at noon on the day that the Conservatives were due to move their vote of no confidence in the government. The Cabinet agreed the pact but there was strong opposition to it from a number of ministers including Tony Benn, Peter Shore and the new Scottish Secretary Bruce Millan. Labour won the no confidence motion by 322 votes to 298. The Lib-Lab pact was renewed in July 1977 and was to last until August 1978. During these months Callaghan could afford to relax and concentrate on the positive aspects of being the country's Prime Minister. There was a slight blip over his appointment of his son-in-law Peter Jay as the ambassador to the United States. Jay was married to Callaghan's daughter Margaret, later, as Baroness Jay, to be Leader of the House of Lords under Tony Blair. The appointment brought cries of nepotism but the reality was that David Owen had recommended Jay for the position. However, Callaghan should have foreseen the likely reaction to this appointment, and, given the unpopularity of the government with the voters, asked himself if it was worth inviting flak for.

President Carter paid a state visit to Britain between 5 and 7 May then Callaghan chaired the Third World Economic Summit in Downing Street with the leaders of the USA, France, Germany, Italy, Canada and Japan. The following month brought the celebrations surrounding the Queen's Silver Jubilee celebrations and a meeting of the Commonwealth Heads of Government meeting in London over which Callaghan presided. During this meeting Callaghan took the Heads of State north by train to Gleneagles, the five-star hotel set in the Perthshire countryside. It was here that the Gleneagles Agreement was reached which excluded South Africa from sporting contacts with Commonwealth countries. It was proving to be somewhat of an idyllic summer for Callaghan as he then had successful meetings with the TUC Economic

Committee on the continuance of pay restraint. Although not as formal as previous agreements, the TUC issued a statement on 19 July calling on affiliates to avoid a pay explosion and warning of the economic problems which could be caused if wage increases were to go beyond 10 per cent. This statement was endorsed at the TUC meeting in September, and Callaghan had succeeded in securing another major part of the jigsaw aimed at solving Britain's economic problems.

The country was moving from the dark shadows of hyper-inflation to bask in the warmer climes of economic prosperity. Inflation was still running at 17 per cent but was predicted to come down to 8.5 per cent by January 1978. The pound was rising against the dollar and when it reached $1.80 the Bank of England found itself reversing its normal role of recent years. Instead of having to defend Sterling the Bank was selling Sterling to prevent it rising further but it still rose to over $1.90. By mid-September reserves had reached $14.85 billion and the FT 30 Share Index reached a record level of 592.2 on 14 September. Other economic data was equally encouraging. The third quarter of 1977 recorded a £483 million surplus while August saw the largest ever surplus in one month of £316 million.

The government's desire to keep wage increases to the 10 per cent level recommended by the TUC was challenged when the Fire Brigades Union presented a claim to their local government employers of 30 per cent and a reduction in their working week to 42 hours. Callaghan met the union's general secretary Terry Parry along with the union's executive on 29 November to tell them that the government could not allow them to succeed in their claim. The strike continued and the government were forced to mobilise 20,000 troops and bring Second World War fire engines out of mothballs. The vehicles quickly became known as 'Green Goddesses' because of their all-green colouring and troops were given basic training in fire-fighting. The strike lasted until the end of January 1978 but the government's line on pay held, although the firemen won their 42-hour week.

While the fire brigade strike was in progress the power workers made a similar demand for a 30 per cent increase accompanied with threatening noises of strike action which would have led to widespread blackouts in industry and homes. The employers offered 10 per cent but on 2 February the union rejected this and eventually a settlement averaging 17 per cent was reached on 2 April. Both these claims were early signs of the difficulty in delivering wage restraint for the third year running.

As 1977 drew to a close Callaghan had two meetings with the Israeli Prime Minister Menachem Begin, leader of the Likud Party, at Chequers, about the possible withdrawal by Israel from Sinai. The following month, January 1978, on his way from a visit to India, Pakistan and Bangladesh, Callaghan stopped over in Cairo to meet the Egyptian President Anwar Sadat and discussed the position of the West Bank, passing on Sadat's views to President Carter who was making a determined effort to broker a peace deal in the Middle East. The result was that in September 1978 the Camp David Agreement was signed between Egypt and Israel. Under the terms of the agreement Egypt regained Sinai and in return recognised the State of Israel. Callaghan could claim some credit for the part he played in helping to bring this agreement about. President Carter used the British Prime Minister as a sounding board on Middle East politics.

Closer to home the Labour government, still getting accustomed to being a member of the European Community, were suddenly faced with proposals for even closer European links. The suggestion was that the members of the EC should form a European Monetary System to prevent exchange rate fluctuations between members with the prospect of it leading to a European single currency at a later date. The idea was first mooted at a breakfast Callaghan had at the French embassy with the German Chancellor Schmidt and the French President during a European Council meeting in Copenhagen on 8 April. Callaghan in his memoirs said that he favoured the concept in principle but that because of the opposition in Britain and also the high exchange rate of Sterling he did not believe that Britain could join such a system at least at the outset.

The subject was returned to at a further meeting of the European Heads of Government in Bremen in July. The Cabinet discussed the proposals at a number of Cabinet meetings during November and December 1978 but decided that it was premature to arrive at a decision. During the Thatcher years Britain did join the ERM in October 1990 at what ironically was to prove to be too high an exchange rate, the very fear that Callaghan had expressed 12 years earlier. This resulted in Britain withdrawing from the system in September 1992.

There were many positive signs which Labour could feel pleased about, particularly on the economic front, and Callaghan, despite his government's precarious position in the Commons, had established himself as a statesman on the international stage. However in August 1978 the Liberals ended the Lib-Dem pact and Callaghan believed that in order to complete the repair work to the economy a fourth year of pay restraint was required which coupled with devolution was to spell the end of his government but could he have avoided it?

Chapter 8: The Election that Never Happened

Perhaps the most significant event of Callaghan's term as Prime Minister was the general election that never happened, at least when it was supposed to happen. The nation expected Callaghan to announce the date of a general election to be held the following month when he made a prime-ministerial broadcast on the evening of Thursday 7 September 1978. Instead the Prime Minister explained why he was NOT calling a general election. I watched the broadcast in the company of the staff of the Labour Party in Scotland and the reaction from the Scottish Secretary, Helen Liddell was one of stunned silence. Election preparations had already begun. I had been given leave of absence from my position as Financial Correspondent of the *Daily Record* to handle the press relations for the campaign. I had already been *in situ* in Keir Hardie House in Glasgow for a fortnight. I had returned to the office to watch the broadcast from a meeting with Bob Gillespie, a SOGAT official, who had agreed that his branch would donate £5,000 towards Labour's election campaign. Now we were told there was to be no general election, at least not in 1978. How this came about is unclear. The decision was certainly Jim Callaghan's but how he arrived at it, and when, is open to debate.

Tentative planning for a general election had started as far back as July 1977. Some argued that there was an advantage in waiting until the spring of 1979 when the new voters' register would be operational, and this was thought to be worth up to six seats for Labour. In the first half of 1978 Labour Party staff had begun to assemble a campaign team and on 19 May this team held its first meeting under the chairmanship of Derek Gladwin an official of the General and Municipal Workers' Union. Cabinet members Michael Foot and Merlyn Rees were members of the committee as was Norman Willis from the TUC and Mike Malloy of the *Daily Mirror*. There was a growing feeling that the general election should be called for October. There were two main considerations to be taken into account – devolution and the question of pay restraint. Both were eventually to play major roles in bringing down the Labour government.

Devolution had been moribund ever since the government had suffered a defeat in the Commons in February 1977 when it failed to impose a guillotine on the bill. The issue was re-invigorated when the Lib-Lab pact was formed. The Liberals, as part of the agreed package had secured Labour's agreement that they would re-introduce devolution in two separate Bills, one for Scotland the other for Wales. Michael Foot and John Smith had been given the task of bringing the new Bills forward. The Bills were put before Parliament in November 1978 but again ran into opposition, not only from Conservatives but also from within the ranks of Labour MPs. Scottish Labour MP Tam Dalyell raised what is to this day known as the West Lothian question when he asked how Scottish MPs sitting in the Commons could vote on issues which had been devolved to the Scottish Parliament allowing them to vote on policies which would only apply in England and Wales while the English MPs had no say in devolved matters. The most immediate problem was created when George Cunningham, a Scot who represented the London seat of Islington South and Finsbury, put forward an amendment to the Scottish Bill which required 40 per cent of the total electorate to vote in favour of devolution in the referendum before the Bill could be enacted. This effectively counted all those who did not vote in the referendum as No votes, making delivering devolution in Scotland more difficult. George Cunningham's amendment was carried by 15 votes despite government opposition. The division within the Labour ranks on the devolution issue was highlighted by the fact that more than 30 Labour MPs voted for the amendment. The Acts delivering devolution to Scotland and Wales were given the Royal Assent on 31 July two days before the House rose for the summer recess. The smoking gun was now loaded lying in wait for the government. Dates for the referenda had now to be fixed before the Acts could be put into force.

I ceased to worship free collective bargaining more than 10 years ago.

CALLAGHAN

While the Commons debated the devolution issue, Callaghan was carrying on another debate outside the Commons on the issue of pay restraint. Callaghan believed that there had to be another year of wage restraint with a fixed norm. In December 1977 Callaghan revealed his approach to wage negotiations for the following year when he told Parliament: *I ceased to worship free collective bargaining more than 10 years ago.*[1] He arrived at the figure of 5 per cent very soon after making this statement, mentioning the figure in a BBC radio interview on 1 January 1978. The Prime Minister was determined that inflation should be kept in single figures, having fallen from an average of 15.9 per cent during 1977 to a predicted 8.5 per cent for 1978. He paid little heed to the fact that for some months senior trade union leaders had been warning that that they could not deliver wage restraint for a fourth successive year. There are some who suggest that Callaghan believed that with the economic indicators pointing to real improvements in the economy he could appeal over the heads of the trade union leaders directly to union members. He was not attuned to the feelings of grass-roots union members. As a member of the National Executive of the National Union of Journalists at the time, and also as Convener of Shop Stewards in the *Daily Record* and *Sunday Mail* plant in Scotland it was obvious to me that shop floor patience with pay restraint had reached breaking point. In the newspaper industry there was little sign of restraint. Readers were still being asked to pay more for their papers, and advertisers were facing rate increases. The main beneficiaries of wage restraint appeared to be the owners, who enjoyed higher profits. The feeling of injustice was heightened by the results of a 'Top Peoples" salary review chaired by Lord Boyle. The body recommended increases averaging 30 per cent for already highly paid judges and senior civil servants which the Cabinet was divided on, but Callaghan accepted it while admitting that he realised this could cause problems. Why Callaghan acted in this way when there was so much at stake is difficult to understand: certainly none of the recipients of the Boyle award would have felt any financial hardship if they had received 5 per cent in line with what the rest of the working population was expected to accept.

In June Callaghan met TUC leaders and bluntly told them that single-figure pay increases were essential and put forward once again the 5 per cent but this time with another 2 per cent to deal with anomalies. The following month the government published a White Paper, 'Winning the Battle Against Inflation', in which 5 per cent was set down as the norm with self-financing productivity agreements also available. The June balance of payments had shown a £224 million surplus and many people believed that this strengthened the logic for calling an October election. His close political advisor Tom McNally thought he was moving towards an October election.

Callaghan retired to his farm at the beginning of August to contemplate on when to call the general election. In his memoirs he describes how many Cabinet members contacted him with their advice, the majority favouring October, but he noted that only one of them had stated that Labour would win. Bernard Donoughue sent him details of various opinion polls. Callaghan recalls how he did his own calculations and came up with Labour on 303 seats, the Conservatives 304 seats. Callaghan did not relish the thought of another hung Parliament and came to the conclusion that the general election should not be called until the Spring of 1979, and went to a 1979 calendar and put a ring round 5 April, the last day of the tax year. He visited Healey at his home nearby in Sussex and informed the Chancellor of his decision.

Inexplicably, having stated that he had made his decision, Callaghan at the end of August asked all the Cabinet members to give their opinion at the beginning of September on when a general election should be called. His official biographer Kenneth O Morgan stated in his biography of Callaghan that of those Cabinet members who gave written views, ten were in favour of an October election while those against, including the Prime Minister, favoured a spring election.

If this consultation did not indicate hesitancy then it was nothing more than a charade, and when Cabinet members were finally informed of the decision and that it had been taken on 17 August, they were understandably upset. Callaghan continued to play his cards close to his chest, on 1 September, four days before the Prime Minister was due to address Congress, he was host to a number of TUC leaders and General Secretaries at a dinner at Upper Clayhill Farm. The discussion round the dinner table centred on the pros and cons of an October election with most of those present including David Basnett of the GMB, Len Murray, TUC General Secretary, and Terry Duffy of the Engineers favouring an early election. Many of the dinner guests were angered when Callaghan announced on 7 September that he was not calling an election and were further dismayed when it emerged that the decision had already been made before their dinner appointment.

Prior to announcing his decision, Callaghan addressed Congress and gave a strong defence of the need for a 5 per cent wage norm. Delegates were taken aback when during his speech he broke into song, singing: *There was I waiting at the Church ... when I found he'd left me in the lurch ... this is what he wrote, Can't get away to marry you today. My wife won't let me.*[2] Callaghan later said that he intended to imply that an election was being delayed,

'There was I waiting at the Church ... when I found he'd left me in the lurch ... this is what he wrote, Can't get away to marry you today. My wife won't let me.'

CALLAGHAN

but the majority in the TUC drew the opposite conclusion. Certainly the Cabinet was taken aback when on 7 September, the date Callaghan had publicly set aside to make an announcement concerning a general election, when they were informed that he had decided delay until the following year.

That evening Callaghan made a television and radio broadcast to the nation and explained that there would not be a general election in 1978. Millions of viewers and listeners up and down the country were astounded at this turn of events. To this day I find the fact that Callaghan in his own memoirs says that the decision was made in the middle of August difficult to understand. Why, if this was the case, did he sanction the detailed preparatory work for an October election involving the Labour Party organisation? My own involvement began in August when I was approached by the late Stewart MacLauchlan, the Scottish Political Editor of the *Daily Record*, which was part of the *Mirror* stable of newspapers. He asked if I would handle the press matters for Keir Hardie House, the Scottish HQ of the Labour Party, for the duration of the forthcoming general election. I agreed and the next week was installed in an office there. Jim Rodger, a sports writer for the *Daily Mirror* in Scotland who had contacts at the highest levels of the party, took me to the Central Hotel in Glasgow. Jim introduced me to the manager and explained to me that he had booked an entire floor of the hotel in his name on behalf of the Prime Minister on the night he was launching the general election campaign in Glasgow. It had become a Labour Party tradition that election campaigns were launched in Glasgow. He then, from the foyer of the hotel phoned Number 10 Downing Street and put Bernard Donoughue on to me. Donoughue promised to provide me with whatever assistance I needed.

The Campaign Office in London was already in the process of organising a contract with printers in Plymouth to print an election newspaper for the entire UK. Any constituency party who wished could have their candidate's message along with a photograph on the front page. I intervened immediately I heard this and persuaded them to allow the Scottish editions to be printed in Scotland. I explained that it would be impossible for the papers to be sent from Plymouth to Glasgow and then circulated to individual constituencies in the time allotted for a general election campaign. I then negotiated a Scottish contract with printers in Irvine, Ayrshire. Other staff in the office were busy preparing constituency organisations for the campaign. It was all systems go! Then came the 7 September broadcast which left us all stunned. We adjourned to a nearby wine bar and let the drink and the adrenaline flowing from us bring us down to earth. Why were the campaign preparations allowed to go so far down the road if the Prime Minister had already decided against an October election? I would have understood if some preparatory work had been allowed to go ahead to wrong-foot the opposition, but to book hotel rooms in secret, to place contracts with printers and bring in additional staff is puzzling.

The die, however, was cast. Although Callaghan had arrived at his decision after consulting the Cabinet, senior trade union figures and the senior members of his staff, he did not go along with the views of the majority. The decision was his. He made it while on his farm after working out how he believed each constituency result would go. He then visited his Chancellor, not to take advice but to inform him of the decision he had taken. His government now had the autumn and winter to survive in the Commons without the cushion of the Lib-Lab pact when all the signs were suggesting major problems on the industrial front.

Chapter 9: 'The Winter of Discontent'

Throughout his political career Callaghan had given every sign that he had never forgotten the basic lessons he had learned as a trade union official. However, as 1978 approached there were signs that the Prime Minister was now committing one of the cardinal sins of any leader. He was not listening

From the very outset, when Callaghan had raised the 5 per cent norm, he had met with scepticism. Even Healey who had worked closely with him in the previous three years of wage restraint cautioned on being too dogmatic, and few, if any, of the trade union leaders expressed the belief that such a target was achievable. It would not have come as a surprise to Callaghan when the Labour Party Conference in Blackpool (2–6 October) rejected the proposed wage restraint by 4 million votes to 1.9 million. Callaghan, however, should have been alerted to trouble ahead by the fact that Terry Duffy, President of the Amalgamated Union of Engineering Workers, speaking as a delegate for the Liverpool Wovertree Labour Party Constituency was the mover of the motion which called for the government to 'immediately cease intervening in wage negotiations'. Duffy described the 5 per cent norm as 'political suicide'.

From my own personal experience both as a shop steward and a member of the NUJ executive council the 5 per cent norm being put forward was unacceptable. The consensus within the trade union movement was that if the government had been more flexible and allowed for a range of settlements of between 5 per cent and 8 per cent then another year of wage restraint might have been accepted. Inflation was running at 8 per cent and a 5 per cent norm would have meant another real cut in living standards. The mood in the union ranks was that they would not accept 5 per cent being imposed on them. This was not a case of militant leaders fomenting trouble. The leadership at plant level was responding to their members' refusal to go along with a 5 per cent wage ceiling. The past three years had been a testing time for union grass-root leaders. They had had a difficult time convincing members on the shop floor to go along with the voluntary wage restraint packages. Of course the social contract with the government had softened the impact and was a major factor in the movement's co-operation, but it had not been a smooth passage. I had visited the TUC in London on several occasions to try and persuade them to accept that our wage formula allowed us to receive higher than the agreed norm of that particular year. The TUC and the individual trade union leaders deserve thanks for the part they played in reducing inflation. Instead they have been blamed for bringing down the Labour government. This, I believe, is a too simplistic analysis of the events which led up to Labour's downfall. Frank Chapple, the right-wing General Secretary of the Electrical Trades Union had this to say in his memoirs *Sparks Fly* about the 5 per cent norm and the decision to delay the general election: 'Callaghan, pressed to hang on by Michael Foot, had gravely misjudged the union mood and those of us who feared the worst were proved correct. It took no great foresight – which made the Prime Minister's decision all the more remarkable.'[1]

The immediate reaction to Callaghan's announcement that

there would be no general election in 1978 saw a surge in favour of Labour in the opinion polls. In his autobiography, Callaghan noted: *Taking one month with another, the Opinion Polls were oscillating, pointing in no consistent direction, but it seemed not unreasonable to assume that the Government, having made such a remarkable recovery in public estimation from our abysmal showing of two years earlier, would have good hopes of consolidating public confidence by the spring of 1979 and even prospects of scoring an outright victory.* He then added: *But the winter of discontent intervened, and I must ... give some account of those events that were to shatter our hopes and antagonise the country beyond recall.*[2] Indeed at the beginning of November a hint of what lay ahead came with a bakers' strike which led to bread rationing and Callaghan stated publicly that the winter was 'make or break time' for the government.

The Transport and General Workers Union had submitted whopping claims of 30 per cent for their 150,000 members employed by Ford and British Leyland and a 40 per cent claim for their members in the road haulage industry. At the end of September Ford workers rejected a 5 per cent wage offer and withdrew their labour. After a lengthy stoppage the company finally offered 17 per cent, three times higher than the government's 5 per cent norm. This became the marker for other groups of workers. No sooner had the Ford workers returned to work than oil tanker drivers threatened to take action in support of their 40 per cent claim. The threat of strike action proved to be enough and as Christmas neared they accepted an average 20 per cent pay rise. Earlier in December a government proposal to impose financial penalties on Ford and other companies for ignoring the government's guidelines was defeated by 285 votes to 279 with several Labour MPs abstaining. Any illusion of an effective wage restraint policy had disappeared.

An angry Prime Minister retired to Chequers for the Christmas break before flying to Guadeloupe on 4 January 1979 for a four-power summit with the US, France and West Germany. Immediately prior to his departure news that a road haulage strike had began in Scotland had reached him, and as he flew out the situation grew worse with the strike spreading to England and Wales. The French Caribbean Island in the West Indies was chosen because of its isolated position which would allow the leaders to meet away from the normal media attention which normally descends on meetings such as these. The leaders were accompanied by their wives and were able to conduct their business in a relaxed setting. The agenda was wide ranging but the main item was the SALT II talks between the US and the Soviet Union. President Carter was anxious to reach a settlement on SALT II which dealt with the number of strategic nuclear long-range weapons both countries held. The Russians however had developed SS20 missiles, weapons which were mobile and would be targeted on the major cities of European NATO members. These weapons were not covered in the SALT II talks. The West German Chancellor Helmut Schmidt had expressed his concern that if the two superpowers reached an agreement on long-range weapons this would still leave Europe vulnerable to the new SS20 and in particular West Germany which was in the front line. Carter was willing to deploy Pershing II and Tomahawk cruise missiles in Europe but before committing the US to the costs involved wanted assurances that European NATO members would be willing to have these missiles on their soil. No firm agreement was reached on this issue during the two days of talks.

Callaghan took the opportunity of the Guadeloupe summit to have private talks with Carter about Britain's future as a nuclear power. The Polaris submarine-launched ballistic missile would become obsolete in the 1990s and if it was to be replaced by the next generation of nuclear weapons a decision would have to be made in the near future. He discussed with Carter the possibility of Britain purchasing its successor Trident, and the US President indicated that he did not foresee any problems with this. Callaghan made it clear that the British Cabinet had not reached any firm conclusion on whether it would remain a nuclear power. While Callaghan was engaged in these talks the industrial situation back home was rapidly deteriorating. The average British household was more concerned with having their rubbish collected, their sick children treated and the dead buried than they were about SALT II talks or the country's future as a nuclear power. The choice of Guadeloupe as a media-free haven had proved highly successful. The effect of this was that the media had little concrete to report on other than that the four leaders were ensconced on a Caribbean island with their wives. This meant that as far as the British press was concerned there was little news to compete with the stories of the industrial strife sweeping Britain. Indeed the impression was often given in sections of the press that the Prime Minister was enjoying some kind of foreign junket in the sunshine of the Caribbean while the British population had to endure the cold British winter surrounded by anarchy. The Guadeloupe summit ended on 6 January but the Prime Minister had agreed to stop-over in Barbados on his way home. The decision to go ahead with this part of the itinerary

I don't think other people in the world share the view that there is mounting chaos.

CALLAGHAN

at a time when the country was facing industrial havoc has to be questioned. In Liverpool grave-diggers refused to bury the dead, there were food shortages brought about by the road haulage strike and panic buying, and many families were finding it difficult to heat their homes because heating oil was not being delivered.

Callaghan finally arrived back in London on 10 January. On the flight home the Prime Minister made an unwise and ill-advised decision to hold a press conference at Heathrow immediately upon his arrival. He had not given himself time to fully recover from a long flight or to become attuned to the political climate before facing the media. When asked by a reporter from an *Evening Standard* about the chaos caused by the widespread industrial action Callaghan replied: *I don't think other people in the world share the view that there is mounting chaos*. The following day's edition of the *Sun* newspaper interpreted this as the Prime Minister saying 'Crisis? What Crisis?[3] The perception was that these were the words of the Prime Minister. This headline was to haunt Callaghan and no matter how unfairly, reinforced the impression of his being out of touch. The mistake had been in holding the press conference when he was not fully prepared for it. The country was soon to be engulfed in strikes which appeared to be infectious, spreading from one industry to another with industrial action being taken in a variety of industries including, rail, water and sewage while secondary picketing at ports and depots prevented goods from being distributed. Public sector workers added to the problem with a series of stoppages bringing chaos to schools, ambulance services and hospitals.

Callaghan appeared to be like a rabbit caught in a car's headlights. Little action appeared to be taken by Number 10 Downing Street for the remainder of January. Callaghan's traditional allies in the trade union movement Hugh Scanlon and Jack Jones had both retired. Their successors Terry Duffy and Moss Evans did not carry the same weight or influence nor were they as prepared to co-operate in the fight against inflation. Moss Evans's action in making the haulage drivers' strike official as well as the earlier Ford strike was particularly unhelpful.

The 'Winter of Discontent' reached its peak on 22 January when the TGWU, GMWU, NUPE and COHSE organised a day of action calling out a million and a half workers in support of a £60 a week minimum pay for public service workers. The groundwork, however, had begun to be laid which was to gradually bring the winter of discontent to an end. On 16 January the government had relaxed the 5 per cent pay limit for those earning less than £44.50 a week. Comparability was also introduced to provide a means by which some public employees could achieve more than 5 per cent. The powers of the Price Commission were strengthened to prevent companies automatically passing on the cost of wage increases to consumers. It was the more flexible approach that Healey had suggested earlier but Callaghan had ruled out. If it had been adopted earlier then perhaps the 'Winter of Discontent' might have been avoided.

The effects of the industrial unrest continued to be felt. At the end of January the Health Secretary David Ennals announced that 1,100 of the 2,300 National Health Service hospitals were only carrying out emergency operations. In a desperate bid to reach some form of agreement with the TUC, Callaghan met the entire TUC General Council on 29 January and, while apparently accepting that attempting to keep pay increases within 5 per cent may have been a mistake, he insisted that some form of restraint was required. The TUC leaders were in a more contemplative mood as some of them had been shocked at the ferocity of some of the picket lines and also the backlash in public opinion against trade unions. Callaghan suggested that the government and the TUC should examine together the need to bring inflation down and also to issue guidelines on how future disputes should be conducted. Two working parties were established which allowed Callaghan and TUC General Secretary Len Murray to unveil a concordat on 14 February which would aim to bring inflation down to 5 per cent within three years and the TUC would issue guidance to unions on how strikes were to be conducted and essential services maintained. The government would also sit down with both sides of industry to make an annual assessment of the economy. The St Valentine's Day concordat was to be included in Labour's manifesto at the general election.

The 'Winter of Discontent' slowly petered out, and industrial peace was restored but not before a great deal of damage had been done to the economy, trade unions and the Labour government. The actions carried out in the name of trade unionism did untold damage to the standing of the trade unions which were seen to act in an selfish manner with no regard to what suffering their actions caused. The local authority workers' action came to an end on 21 February when the employees accepted an 11 per cent basic increase plus the opportunity for further increases following a comparability study. Callaghan was disturbed by the disregard shown to the wider community. He continued to believe in consensus politics and reaching voluntary agreements with the trade union movement but the public's trust in trade unions had been damaged.

The industrial strife over, Callaghan now hoped his government would be able to survive in the Commons until the autumn when he had to call a general election in any event. He hoped in the intervening months that the economy would continue to recover and people's memories of the troubled winter would fade. Unfortunately for Labour he was not to have this time. The referendums on Scottish and Welsh devolution were to take place on 1 March and the antipathy of Labour MPs towards devolution which saw them support George Cunningham's 40 per cent amendment was to prove to be Labour's downfall. It was not only in the Commons that Labour was split. There was also a split in Scotland among Labour activists who were allowed to campaign for either the Yes campaign or the No campaign. Among those against devolution were many Labour councillors who believed that their council positions would be downgraded if a Scottish Assembly was to be established. They believed that an Assembly based in Edinburgh would take powers away from them. Prominent Scottish Labour MPs such as the late Robin Cook, Bob Hughes, and Adam Ingram as well as Tam Dalyell were on the No side. Prominent Labour activists such as Brian Wilson and Anne McGuire were also campaigning on the No side. On the Yes side were MPs such as David Lambie and Denis Canavan. Prior to the vote Callaghan travelled north to Scotland to address a Labour Party rally in Glasgow which was presided over by Janey Buchan, chair of the Labour Party in Scotland. Janey, who was married to Labour Party MP, Norman Buchan had strong anti-devolutionist views and managed to make the introductory speech and chair the conference without mentioning devolution once. It was a low-key affair, neither Callaghan nor Scottish Secretary Bruce Millan delivered what could be described as rousing speeches. The No campaign was supported by many industrialists who helped to finance it.

In terms of national politics the Welsh referendum was not as important as there was a clear divide within the Welsh public with many of the anglicised residents of Wales in the south and east of the country being against devolution. A No vote in Wales however was not expected to have any direct impact on the government. Scotland was much more committed. Opinion polls in Scotland had shown a consistent majority in favour of devolution but as a result of the 40 per cent amendment even if the majority taking part in the referendum voted in favour of devolution it would not be delivered unless the total of Yes votes equalled 40 per cent of the entire electorate. In effect this meant that those who did not cast a vote would have their votes counted as a No.

The normal pattern in an election campaign is for every party to attempt to maximise the turnout, but in Scotland's devolution referendum there was an incentive for Labour Party activists against the policy not to campaign. In the Cathcart constituency I belonged to this resulted in the lowest-key campaign I have ever witnessed. My wife Margaret and I along with our three children turned up to hand out leaflets at polling stations but at the Constituency Party rooms in the Castlemilk housing estate in Glasgow there was little activity. I cannot recall meeting a single local councillor on polling day. Despite the deliberately created apathy among Labour party workers on polling day, there was still a 62.9 per cent turnout with 51.6 per cent voting in favour of devolution. If this had been the percentage voting No in the Common Market referendum it would have been enough to take us out of the EC but it was not enough to give Scotland a Scottish Assembly. There can be no doubt that what also affected the Yes vote was the unpopularity of the government with the referendum being held while memories were still fresh of the winter chaos. Referendums have often been used by the electorate to express their views on matters which are not the ostensible subject being decided upon. In Wales the majority voted against devolution in a 59 per cent turnout.

Callaghan was left with little option but to go to the Commons on 22 March and repeal the Scotland Act which immediately led to a no confidence motion being placed before the Commons on 28 March. Labour lost the vote by the narrowest of margins, 311 to 310. Tories, Liberals and SNP all voted against Labour. Jim Sillars and John Robertson voted with the government. Callaghan was wearied by the constant struggle to keep the government afloat at the same time as struggling to maintain some vestige of wage restraint. Michael Foot and others suggested several formulas by which he could perhaps avoid the no confidence vote or attract support from some of the fringe political parties, but the Prime Minister did not appear to have the heart for continued wheeling and dealing and instead chose to face his opponents head-on.

The outcome of the vote was decided by the serious illness of Labour MP Alfred Broughton. Callaghan did not want the sick MP to be subjected to the ordeal of being brought to the Commons by ambulance (he was to die a few days later). SDLP member Gerry Fitt, who had previously supported the Labour government on numerous occasions, was angry at Callaghan's agreement to increase the number of Northern Ireland constituencies and voted against the government. The following day the Cabinet agreed to ask the Queen to dissolve Parliament and for a general election to called on 3 May.

The general election was now on for real. I found myself back at Keir Hardie House as the Party's Press Officer, picking up where I had left off in September the previous year. Callaghan launched the election campaign by addressing a rally in Glasgow. I met him in his room before the rally, and he was in good spirits, looking relaxed and confident, but then he knew that in Scotland Labour still had strong support and that he was going to receive a rapturous welcome when he appeared on the platform. The party in Scotland was well-prepared for the campaign as was proven when 43 constituencies ordered 1.2 million copies of *Labour News* to be distributed to every home in these constituencies. Callaghan delivered a message to voters on the front page of the election newspaper which clearly showed that he stood firmly behind government by consensus. He told the voters: *We will use the oil wealth of the North Sea to create jobs especially for young people.* He laid great store by the St Valentine's Day concordat, writing: *We have cut inflation in half over the last three years. Now we plan to halve price rises again over the next three years. We will attack the Common Market's policy on dear food. We will use the Price Commission to stop unjustified increases. We will develop our agreement with the TUC to raise real income while gradually reducing wage inflation.* He committed the next Labour government to deliver devolution and predicted that *the Tories would turn Scotland into an industrial wasteland by axing the jobs programme.* Once again emphasising his consensus approach to politics, Callaghan promised: *Labour will use our new Standing Commission on Pay Comparability to guarantee a fair pay deal for millions in the public service industries especially the low paid.*[4] The Standing Commission had been established by Callaghan on 26 March under the chairmanship of Professor Hugh Clegg of Warwick University.

The Labour Party manifesto, 'Labour's Way is the Better Way', was a moderate document which Callaghan had fought hard for, refusing to accept the abolition of the House of Lords to be included in it. It is another irony of changing attitudes that a New Labour government some 25 years later should find public opinion favourable to the removal of hereditary peers. However, in 1979 such a proposal would have been portrayed as Labour fighting the Class War. The manifesto did include a promise of 3 per cent growth and a reduction in inflation to 5 per cent.

The battle lines were drawn, Callaghan looking towards voluntary agreements with the TUC and using the Price

Commission and the Pay Comparability approach to convince people to accept lower wage increases while Opposition Leader Margaret Thatcher extolled the free market approach. The stakes were high. Whoever was to form the next government would have the revenues from North Sea oil to bolster their coffers and see a massive boost to the balance of payments as in 1980 the country became a net energy exporter.

The campaign in Scotland went well but the reports coming from the London HQ were not so positive, and there were concerns within the party about the overall result come the 2 May polling date. On the Saturday before polling Callaghan returned to Scotland to address a rally in Edinburgh. He was staying in the North British Hotel attached to Waverley Station where I met him with Alf Young, the Research Officer for the Party in Scotland who had assisted me in preparing campaign leaflets. It was agreed that the Prime Minister would delay his arrival at Leith Town Hall to allow the TV cameras to film the expected enthusiastic welcome. This led to some comedy at the start of the meeting as the Party Chair opened the rally and continued with his prepared speech as if Jim Callaghan was sitting beside him instead of an empty chair, but the laughing soon stopped when Callaghan arrived on the platform and began his address. The 'Troops Out' movement, who had harassed Callaghan throughout the campaign calling for British troops to be withdrawn from Northern Ireland, had infiltrated the meeting. They were well organised and had positioned themselves around the hall inevitably sitting in the centre of the rows. They did not all heckle at once. Instead one of their numbers would disrupt the meeting while the rest remained silent. Once this person had been removed from the hall, another would start, and so it went on throughout the rally. Callaghan's speech was ruined. The following day's Sunday newspapers were about the disruption, not the content of his speech. Callaghan was angry that the demonstrators had been able to obtain tickets for the event and let his displeasure be known.

The campaign centred round Callaghan and although Labour was behind in the polls, Callaghan was consistently ahead of Margaret Thatcher as the most popular leader. At one point with just a week to go, Labour appeared to be almost neck and neck with the Conservatives but fell back again. Privately Callaghan told Bernard Donoughue towards the end of the campaign: *There are times, perhaps once every thirty years, when there is a sea-change in politics. It then does not matter what you say or what you do. There is a shift in what the public wants and what it approves of. I suspect there is now such a sea-change – and it is for Mrs Thatcher.*[5] The result proved him correct. The final result was Conservatives 339 seats, Labour 268 and Liberals 11. The SNP who had precipitated the election lost nine of their 11 seats and Plaid Cymru one of their three. The Conservatives had 43.9 per cent share of the poll to Labour's 36.9 per cent. Of Labour's 268 seats 44 were in Scotland where they had attracted 42 per cent of the vote. Britain was now divided politically and was to remain so throughout the 18 years of Conservative rule. This was to become known in Scotland as the 'democratic deficit' where Conservative policies, not accepted by the majority of Scottish voters, were imposed on Scotland and the support for devolution ignored. It was this which was to lead to the Labour government elected in 1997 to deliver a Scottish Parliament, not an Assembly, with much stronger powers than proposed by the Callaghan government.

Jim Callaghan was no longer in power, the sea-change

> *There are times, perhaps once every thirty years, when there is a sea-change in politics ... I suspect there is now such a sea-change – and it is for Mrs Thatcher.*
>
> CALLAGHAN

he predicted had happened and Britain was to go through a radical change during the Thatcher years which introduced conviction politics in place of consensus.

Part Three

THE LEGACY

Chapter 10: 'Father of the House'

Following the general election defeat in May 1979 Callaghan's first instinct was to resign as leader of the Labour Party but he was persuaded to stay on and was unanimously re-elected. The hope was that by staying on for a year the bitterness which sweeps any political movement following an election defeat would have ebbed and the political landscape become more suited to Denis Healey being elected as his successor.

With hindsight his decision to stay on was a mistake. The entryists who were determined to take control of the party and convert it into a vehicle for their own brand of socialism showed no respect for Callaghan's many achievements as a servant of the Labour movement for almost 50 years. Callaghan had to suffer personal insults from members of the intelligentsia who believed that they alone knew what was good for the working class. He despaired as Militant Tendency and others such as the Revolutionary Socialist League as well as Maoists tried to gain control of the Labour Party. They targeted poorly-attended constituency parties and trade union branch meetings to capture control of the policymaking bodies of the wider labour movement. My own union, the National Union of Journalists, as a white-collared professional organisation, was also a prime target and I recall a conversation between a Militant member of the National Executive and a Maoist. The Maoist was accusing Militant of being entryists into the Labour Party to which the Militant member replied: 'So are you' to which the Maoist replied 'But we are democratic entryists.' Such was the level of reality.

The reason why Callaghan's decision to remain as leader was a mistake was that the extreme left in the party was poised on several fronts to transform the machinery of the party to their liking. At the Party Conference in October 1979 they won the vote on the reselection of MPs and were pushing for the party leader to be elected by an electoral college and for the National Executive to draw up the manifesto for general elections. Callaghan was against these changes. His only success was, at the 1980 Party Conference, to salvage the Cabinet's responsibility for drawing up the Party Manifesto albeit with the involvement of NEC members.

Callaghan knew that he was merely holding the fort when what was required at this time was a Party Leader fired up to defend the Parliamentary Party against the onslaught of this new-style left who showed little or no sign of being willing to live together in a broad church with those who did not share their precise views of socialism. The 17 months which Callaghan remained as leader were essentially wasted time as the party was torn apart and leading figures such as William Rogers, David Owen and Shirley Williams turned their attention to forming a new centrist political party. If the battle against Militant had started earlier then some defectors may have thought it worthwhile to remain in the Labour Party and fight their corner. In any event the strategy of easing the way for Healey to succeed did not work as Foot defeated Healey in the leadership election. On 15 October 1980 Callaghan returned to the Labour backbenches for the first time in 29 years. He began to speak out in favour of expelling Militant and Tony Benn in his diaries noted: 'Jim Callaghan has a centre spread in the *Mirror* arguing that Labour must expel Militant, prepare for a coalition with the SDP after the election, and consider proportional representation.'[1]

Although Callaghan supported Mrs Thatcher in the Commons in the use of military force to recapture the Falklands in April 1982 he rebuked her for leaving the islands unguarded by removing HMS *Endurance* and when Thatcher claimed that a Labour government would not have fired a shot to recover the islands, Callaghan retorted: *I tell the right hon. Lady, if we had been in power we would not have needed to.*[2] Benn wrote in his diaries: 'Jim Callaghan spoke with absolutely naked support for Mrs Thatcher. He is just an old warmonger. As a former PM he carries a lot of weight but he certainly doesn't speak for the Labour Party.'[3]

In 1983 Callaghan became the Father of the House as the longest-serving member. With this position went the privilege of being able to speak in the Commons whenever he wished, a perk which he took full advantage of and in 1985 he was named the *Spectator*'s Backbencher of the Year in their Parliamentary Awards. Callaghan enjoyed his new-found freedom and used it on occasion to voice his opposition to his own party's unilateral nuclear disarmament policy. One intervention which perhaps should not have been made in the light of an approaching general election was Callaghan's contribution in the Commons on 9 March 1987 when in the defence debate he openly supported Trident, drawing attention to the Labour Party's stance on nuclear weapons. His comments drew criticism from many quarters who were concerned at the damage it could do to Labour at the expected general election. This prompted Benn to write in an unflattering manner in his diaries: 'Jim Callaghan's speech in the House on Monday in support of Trident during the debate on INF has exploded all over the place. It is being said that because Jim never won an election when he was Prime Minister he doesn't see why any other Labour leader should, or that he is really a member of the SDP, or that he has nothing to lose because he is leaving Parliament and is retiring. But he has done great damage, it is always the right wing of the Party that does the damage.'

Callaghan duly retired at the June general election and became a member of the Lords. His departure from the Commons allowed him to spend more time on his farm although he and Audrey retained a house in London only a 10-minute drive from the Houses of Parliament. By 1994 they had ten grandchildren, and two great-grandchildren. He continued to enjoy good health although in January 1985 he had had an operation to remove his gall bladder and in October 1988 he suffered a minor heart attack. His wife too enjoyed good health which allowed both of them to travel widely, including his annual visits to Gerald Ford in Colorado. In all the Callaghans visited almost 40 countries after 1979.

In the Lords Callaghan was a regular contributor and gave evidence in 1994 before the Nolan Committee on standards in public life. Callaghan received many honours in his retirement but unlike others he did not collect directorships or sell his reputation for profit. Instead he concentrated on educational and charitable causes. In 1995 he attended Harold Wilson's funeral in the Scillies and delivered a fond memorial address at Westminster Abbey.

The arrival of Tony Blair as Labour's leader following John Smith's sudden death in May 1994 and the advent of New Labour did not enthuse Callaghan. He refused to be tagged 'Old Labour' by the revisionists who worked to distance New Labour from its working class roots. Instead, according to his biographer Professor Kenneth O Morgan, he preferred to describe himself as 'original' Labour. The Callaghan years are largely ignored by the Blair government. It is to be hoped that in future the role that Callaghan played in the Wilson governments and also when he was Prime Minister himself will be recognised for the valiant fight they put up to keep Britain afloat and also bring down inflation when it was threatening to reach Latin American standards.

In her latter years Lady Callaghan became increasingly frail. Initially her husband insisted on caring for her but he eventually reluctantly agreed that she required professional care although he visited her daily. His wife of 67 years had been a constant companion to him. She had enjoyed her own political career as an alderman in the London Borough of Lewisham and on the Greater London Council but what had given her the most satisfaction was her involvement with the Great Ormond Street Hospital for Children, chairing the board of governors from 1969 until 1982 and was a trustee of their Wishing Well Appeal until 1990. Lady Callaghan died on 15 March 2005 and 11 days later on 26 March Lord Callaghan of Cardiff, the longest-living British prime minister, died at the family's Sussex home on the eve of his 93rd birthday.

Chapter 11: Assessment

History has yet to judge Callaghan in the round. The chaos of the 'Winter of Discontent' appears to be the yardstick by which most commentators judge his political achievements, including his premiership, but these events only account for a period of three months in a political career which spanned almost 35 years.

Callaghan deserves to be judged by weighing his achievements against his failures over his long involvement in British politics during which he held the three great offices of State, Chancellor of Exchequer, Home Secretary and Foreign Secretary, before becoming Prime Minister. When he held the first three offices it was before presidential-style government had come into vogue with the arrival of Margaret Thatcher and Tony Blair. Callaghan was in charge of his departments. Harold Wilson did not try to do his job for him. He was never dealt a good hand. Whatever political post he held crisis appeared to follow. While Chancellor he was bequeathed a massive Balance of Payments deficit by the outgoing Conservative government which provoked a Sterling crisis ending in devaluation; at the Home Office he was faced with the Northern Ireland situation finally coming to the boil after 60 years of simmering; while at the Foreign Office there were the Common Market negotiations and Cyprus. Finally his premiership was plagued by yet another currency crisis and industrial strife.

When passing judgement we have to take into consideration the world that Callaghan lived in. He was not cushioned
by North Sea oil revenues which only began to flow in any
great quantity in the latter months of his premiership.
Margaret Thatcher inherited the benefits of oil. You cannot
judge him by comparing what governments of today would
do. It was a different era. Today the public bemoan the fact
that the Commons is full of professional politicians who have
done little else in life. Callaghan was certainly not of this
type. He left school at 17 and went to work as a clerk in the
Inland Revenue before becoming an active trade unionist and
rising through the ranks to become Assistant Secretary of the
Inland Revenue Staff Federation before volunteering to join
the Royal Navy during the Second World War. It could not
be said of him that he had not experienced life outside the
cloistered world of the Houses of Parliament before he became
an MP in 1945 at the age of 33. He entered Parliament at
a time when Britain was on its knees. Fighting the Second
World War had been an extremely costly affair. The rest of
Europe, including those countries we defeated benefited from
US generosity through the Marshall Plan while Britain was
forced to convert our Lend-Lease arrangement into a massive
loan. Sterling was under pressure from 1945 as the country
fought an economic war to survive.

Critics of Callaghan when examining his period as Chancellor come to the view that he was not the best Chancellor we
have ever had. This may be true but how many other Chancellors came into office and discovered that the preceding
government had left a £800 million deficit in the balance of
payments? This was the position Callaghan found himself
in when Labour won a narrow victory in the October 1964
general election. Most of the criticism directed at Callaghan
and the Wilson government is that they delayed biting the

Callaghan as Premier

Callaghan was not a collective operator in all circumstances. Like his first mentor, Atlee, he kept his nuclear weapons policy inside the narrowest and tightest of circles, away even (unlike Atlee or his second mentor, Wilson) from the Cabinet committee structure. Callaghan's forum was known as the Nuclear Defence Policy Group. He told me that on matters like the replacement of Polaris, 'it was always traditional, and nothing new, for nuclear issues to be discussed in a small group' (plainly unaware of the Churchill model which had embraced the full Cabinet when the decision to make a British hydrogen bomb was taken in 1954).

In a manner that should still be a model for his successors in No. 10, Jim Callaghan laid great stress on keeping personally well-briefed on the small problems which could suddenly flare up and inflame a government – the Falklands, Gibraltar and Belize were the examples he liked to quote. His naval background was the key here. The essence of Callaghan, the ex-navy man and careful keeper of the watch, came over beautifully when he explained this for the viewers of *All the Prime Minister's Men*. He had, he said, 'my own personal source of information. Because of my background, I asked the Admiralty every week to send me a map of the world, about the size of this blotter in front of us here, which set out the position and disposition of every ship in the British navy, including all the auxiliaries, so that I could know exactly what we could do and how long it would take us to get to the Falklands and where we needed to be. That is the kind of thing I think a prime minister must do. There are small things he must do and large things. That's one of the small things he must do that can save a very large catastrophe.' [Peter Hennessy, *The Prime Minister* (Penguin, London: 2000) pp 389–91.]

bullet and devaluing the Pound for too long. It was not until November 1967 that devaluation took place. It is forgotten that having been left with no alternative when taking office to seeking a massive $3,000 million of international aid, Callaghan's strategy to tackle the problem appeared to be working. In the spring of 1967 the Bank Rate was cut to 5.5 per cent and Britain's reserves were rising. Then two major events occurred out of the control of Callaghan – the Six Day War between Israel and Egypt followed by an oil embargo on Britain and then an unofficial dock strike at Britain's major ports damaging our exports. Together these events forced Callaghan and Wilson to propose devaluation. This course of action perhaps should have been considered earlier but Labour had an aversion to becoming synonymous with devaluation.

If Callaghan can be accused of shirking difficult decisions while Chancellor, this is not a criticism which can be made of his period as Home Secretary. Race relations in Britain became a major issue in Britain during his period of office and emotions were running high with Enoch Powell making his infamous 'rivers of blood' speech in Birmingham and East African countries expelling their Asian population, thousands of whom held British passports. Callaghan acted to stem the flow of Asian immigrants into Britain to prevent racial tensions in this country rising and pressure being put on local services where the immigrants settled in this country. He was accused of racism in his handling of this problem and there can be no denying that there was an element of racial discrimination in the legislation Callaghan introduced successfully into the Commons. Indeed the European Commission on Human Rights condemned the policy as discriminatory. Callaghan however could not be accused of being a racist. He was popular with many African Commonwealth leaders, since as shadow spokesman for colonial affairs he fought against moves to give independence to the Central African Federation covering Northern and Southern Rhodesia and Nyasaland while it had a constitution which discriminated against black Africans. Callaghan approached the problem of an influx of Asian immigrants in a pragmatic fashion, accepting the criticism that was directed towards him.

Of his handling of Northern Ireland in 1969 Callaghan admitted in the off-the-record meeting he attended in the 1980s that the government's policy was to try to avoid getting directly involved in Northern Ireland and instead to put pressure on the Stormont government to introduce reforms. In this he is guilty of procrastination, but he shares this guilt with every British government minister who held office since Ireland was partitioned in 1921 and the Stormont government formed. Once he took the decision with Harold Wilson in August 1969 to commit British troops in Northern Ireland he handled the situation admirably, helping to prevent the sectarian temperature from igniting into full-blown civil war. British troops are still involved in the Six Counties, as Callaghan feared they would be, but the alternative at that time was to allow an attempt at ethnic cleansing to take place in the Province. Opportunities to resolve the problem may have been missed since then, but the blame for that cannot be laid at Callaghan's door.

In March 1974 following Labour's victory in the general election Callaghan became Foreign Secretary and once again faced immediate turmoil as Labour was committed to rene-gotiating the terms of Britain's entry into the European Community. Callaghan showed great skill in his handling of these negotiations. He had to take along a divided Cabinet and Parliamentary Labour Party with him while trying to reduce Britain's contributions to the Market budget and also gain entry for Commonwealth producers. Wrongly handled, this issue could have split the Labour Party and brought the government down. He can claim a fair degree of success in his negotiations but what he deserves a great deal of credit for is that he took the Labour Party, both inside the Commons and outside along with him resulting in a massive majority in the referendum, thus securing Britain's long-term future in the EC, which he has not been properly recognised for achieving.

Callaghan was two days away from becoming an OAP when he became Prime Minister following Wilson's resignation and his victory in the Labour Party leadership election on 25 March 1976. Once again on gaining office he found a crisis waiting at the door for him. Again it was the age-old problem with Sterling which successive British governments had toiled against since 'winning' the Second World War on the battlefield but not in the international financial markets. On this occasion Callaghan was Prime Minister while Denis Healey was Chancellor of the Exchequer. Healey approached the problem in the traditional Treasury manner, trying to negotiate the best possible deal from the International Monetary Fund while playing by their rules. Callaghan had seen this too often, and he did not accept that Britain's economic position was as bad as the international markets were making out. He pointed to the financial benefits which were soon to be reaped from North Sea oil. He pointed to the fact that inflation was falling and expected to fall further. Inflation had peaked at 26.9 per cent in August 1975 and was now approaching single figures. He held parallel talks with the US President and the German Chancellor and in a private meeting faced up the IMF. He also pushed for Sterling to no longer be a Reserve Currency. The result was Britain saw off the worse of the cuts which the IMF wished them to impose. The crisis faced by Callaghan's government at that time has been likened to the problems faced by Ramsay

MacDonald in 1931 when the Labour government resigned and a coalition government was formed bringing swingeing cuts in living standards. Callaghan avoided this due to his skills as a political negotiator and his ability to bring a divided Cabinet along with him. Events were to prove him correct. His economic predictions in the main were true but other events and the fact that he led a minority government were to prevent his government from enjoying the spoils that lay ahead of them as the black gold began to gush from the North Sea and Britain became a major oil producer.

Callaghan was a consummate politician. He was not driven by any particular ideology although there is no doubt that he began his political life as a socialist supporting the nationalisation of the major industries by the Atlee government and opposing the terms of the US War Loan which he believed were imposed upon a weakened Britain. He remained a committed trade unionist right to the end of his government and believed in government by consensus attempting to work in partnership with both sides of industry. He did not believe in the free market philosophy in which the strongest prospered and the weakest lost out. He firmly believed in government intervention but by winning over others by force of argument and gaining their co-operation by voluntary methods.

It was these beliefs which led him to oppose Barbara Castle's *In Place of Strife* proposals which would have introduced financial penalties into industrial relations. The cynics accuse him of positioning himself to unseat Wilson but there is no evidence of Callaghan being involved in any plotting against the Prime Minister. His efforts were aimed solely at defeating *In Place of Strife*. He can be criticised for breaching Cabinet collective responsibility during this period, and it could be argued that if he could not accept the policy he should have resigned from the Cabinet but he argued his corner because he felt the proposals would damage both the trade union and labour movements. He paid a political price for his opposition when he was removed from the Inner Cabinet but he remained loyal to his trade union beliefs. He was a politician with principles.

Some have claimed that later events, such as the 'Winter of Discontent', proved that he was wrong to oppose *In Place of Strife*, and that he eventually paid the price for preventing it reaching the statute book. They forget that there had been other attempts to introduce legislation by Edward Heath into industrial relations and they had failed. They also forget that Callaghan's voluntary agreements with the TUC worked for three years, helping to halve inflation. This was an achievement in itself. Perhaps where Callaghan went wrong was when he moved away from the consensus approach and drove through policies without paying too much heed to what was being said around him. This was certainly the case in relation to the 5 per cent norm. He admitted himself that when he first mentioned this figure at a Cabinet meeting in December 1977 it had only just come into his head. There was no discussion beforehand. no consultation with TUC leaders before deciding on the figure. He was assailed on all sides, including by Healey that adopting such a rigid approach was a highly dangerous tactic but he pressed ahead, and the result was the 'Winter of Discontent'.

His other experiment with keeping the decision-making process to himself concerned the timing of the general election. The feeling in the Cabinet, among his advisors and in the TUC leadership favoured an October election. Most could see the industrial dangers which lay ahead as a result of the 5 per cent norm and felt it better to go to the country before the negotiating season reached its peak. Callaghan ignored the advice given to him. Not only that, he was accused of conducting a sham consultation regarding the election date with Cabinet members at the start of September when it later emerged he had made his mind up in August. Together these two decisions were Callaghan's downfall. Perhaps he had become overconfident in his own ability to carry people with him.

Today, the complaint among voters is that they are not presented with a real choice at the polls as the similarity between the two main parties, Labour and Conservative, is so great. This is not a complaint which could have been directed at the 1979 election. It was a clash between two opposites. Callaghan stood solidly behind consensus politics and government actively intervening in the economy through a Prices Commission and a Standing Commission on Pay Comparability to provide a better deal for the low paid. Whilst Mrs Margaret Thatcher stood for government following a free market philosophy with the minimum of government intervention and tax cuts as public expenditure was reduced. Callaghan was soundly defeated and since then there have been attempts to denigrate what is described as the Old Labour approach. New Labour rarely refers to the Callaghan government or indeed the Wilson government. Who is to know, however, if Callaghan's way would not have delivered prosperity to Britain? The stakes at the 1979 election were high. The winner could look forward to decades of revenue from North Sea oil and gas. If Callaghan had had this cushion, perhaps consensus politics would have survived. It should not be forgotten that voluntary agreements with the unions had worked in bringing down inflation. The Conservative slogan during the 1979 campaign was that Labour was 'not working' referring to unemployment which was to rise much higher during the Thatcherite years. Certainly the Falklands War would not have taken place for it was Callaghan who sent

HMS *Endurance* to the Falklands as a warning to Argentina but it was the Thatcher government who withdrew the *Endurance*, sending the wrong signal to the Argentineans who invaded the South Atlantic islands resulting in a terrible loss of life.

There was no hint of sleaze about Callaghan. His own public life proceeded without a blemish. He was, however, perhaps the first personality Prime Minister Britain had enjoyed since Churchill. His style on television was very popular and he attracted descriptions such as 'Sunny Jim' because of his amiable demeanour and relaxed manner when meeting people. During the 1979 election the campaign was centred on him and his personal standing remained high in the polls outstripping Margaret Thatcher. Callaghan points out that Labour did not lose votes in the election but suffered because Conservative voters came out in force and switched back from other parties.

Was he a left-wing or right-wing politician? This is a sub-jective question and it depends who you are comparing him with. If it is Tony Benn then you would say he was right wing, while if it was Tony Blair you would put him on the left. One thing can be said, and that is he was a Labour poli-tician. He never saw the need, or experienced the desire, to add the word 'New' when describing his politics. He said he was Labour, and Labour he remained. There is no doubt that he moved towards the centre of politics in the 1960s having entered Parliament as most new Labour MPs did following the Second World War, supporting a radical socialist agenda. However, under his stewardship the Labour Party established the British North Sea Oil Corporation in Glasgow which held a stake in Britain's oil reserves. Privatisation was not on his agenda so although he had moved to the centre, or what was the centre in the political arena he operated in, he remained in today's terms a left-wing politician.

NOTES

Chapter 1: Early Life

1. James Callaghan, *Time and Chance* (Collins, London: 1987) p 35.

Chapter 2: The Attlee Government

1. Francis Beckett, *Clem Attlee* (Politico's, London: 2000).

Chapter 3: Chancellor of the Exchequer

1. Harold Wilson, *The Labour Government 1964–70* (Penguin Books, Middlesex: 1974) p 24.
2. Anthony Howard (ed), *The Crossman Diaries* (Condensed Edition) (Methuen, London: 1979) p 184, hereafter *Crossman Diaries*.
3. *Crossman Diaries*, p 239.
4. *Crossman Diaries*, p 239.
5. Kenneth O Morgan, *Callaghan, a Life* (Oxford University Press, Oxford: 1997) p 257.
6. *Crossman Diaries*, p 342.
7. Wilson, *The Labour Government 1964–70*, p 486.
8. Callaghan, *Time and Chance*, p 216.
9. Wilson, *The Labour Government 1964–70*, p 587.
10. Callaghan, *Time and Chance*, p 222.
11. David Kynaston, *The Financial Times, a Centenary History* (Viking Adult, London: 1988) p 322.
12. Kynaston, *The Financial Times, a Centenary History*, p 365.
13. Kynaston, *The Financial Times, a Centenary History*, p 365.

Chapter 4: Home Secretary

1. Wilson, *The Labour Government 1964–70*, p 639.
2. Callaghan, *Time and Chance*, p 273.
3. Angela Tuckett, *History of the Scottish Trade Union Congress, The First 80 Years 1897–1977*, p 388.
4. *Crossman Diaries*, p 612.
5. Callaghan, *Time and Chance*, p 275.
6. Callaghan, *Time and Chance*, p 277.
7. Tim Pat Coogan, *The Troubles* (Robert Reinhart Publishers, Boulder, Colorado: 1997) p 52.
8. Coogan, *The Troubles*, p 77.
9. Wilson, *The Labour Government 1964–70*, p 876.

Chapter 5: Foreign Secretary

1. Henry Kissinger, *Years of Renewal* (Simon & Schuster, New York: 2000) p 208.
2. Kissinger, *Years of Renewal*, p 209.
3. Callaghan, *Time and Chance*, p 315.

Chapter 6: Prime Minister

1. Kynaston, *The Financial Times, A Centenary History*, p 431.
2. Callaghan, *Time and Chance*, p 418.
3. Callaghan, *Time and Chance*, p 426.
4. 'The Day the £ Nearly Died', *Sunday Times* (1978).

Chapter 7: The Lib-Lab Pact

1. *The Times*, Thursday, 24 March 1977.

Chapter 8: The Election that Never Happened

1. Morgan, *Callaghan, A Life*, p 633.
2. Morgan, *Callaghan, A Life*, p 642.

Chapter 9: 'The Winter of Discontent

1. Frank Chapple, *Sparks Fly* (Michael Joseph Ltd, London: 1985).
2. Callaghan, *Time and Chance*, p 518.
3. Morgan, *Callaghan, A Life*, p 662.
4. Front page of *Labour News* published by the Labour Party in Scotland for the 1979 general election.
5. Morgan, *Callaghan*, A Life, p 697.

Chapter 10: 'Father of the House'

1. Tony Benn, *The End of an Era: Diaries 1980–90* (Arrow, London: 1994) Thursday, 10 December 1981
2. Morgan, *Callaghan, A Life*, p 725.
3. Benn, *The End of an Era*, Thursday, 29 April 1982.

CHRONOLOGY

Year	Premiership
1976	5 April: James Callaghan becomes Prime Minister aged 64. September: Government seeks IMF loan due to sterling crisis. November: IMF negotiating team arrive. December: Chancellor Healey announces terms of IMF loan.
1977	January: Reduction in Minimum Lending Rate. March: Budget announces £2.3 billion in tax cuts. Callaghan visits new US President Carter. Lib-Lab Pact formed, allowing government to win no confidence vote. Queen's Silver Jubilee. November: Fire Brigade Union strike begins.
1978	January: Fire Brigade strike ends. Callaghan meets Egyptian President Sadat before Camp David meeting. April: EC leaders decide to establish the ERM. September: Callaghan announces no general election this year. Scots and Welsh devolution bills. Lib-Lab Pact ends.
1979	January: wave of public service strikes begin – the 'Winter of Discontent', while Callaghan at summit meeting on Guadeloupe. February: Government and TUC announce Concordat bringing 'Winter of Discontent' to an end. March: Scots and Welsh devolution referendums. Government loses no confidence motion by one vote and calls general election. 4 May: Conservatives win general election. Callaghan leaves office, just over three years after he assumed it.

History	Culture
India and Pakistan normalise diplomatic relations. North and South Vietnam are formally unified. Mao Zedong dies. Jimmy Carter (Democrat) wins US presidential election.	Pop group Abba become Sweden's biggest export earner after Volvo. Brotherhood of Man win the Eurovision Song Contest for the UK. Alex Haley, *Roots*. Films: *Marathon Man. Rocky*. TV: *Open All Hours*.
USA and Panama sign the Panama Canal Treaty which returns the canal zone to Panama. Egyptian President Sadat visits Israel and addresses the Knesset.	The Clash, *The Clash*. The Sex Pistols, *God Save the Queen*. Steven Berkoff, *East*. Elvis Presley dies. Films: *Annie Hall. Star Wars. Close Encounters of the Third Kind*.
Communist and Islamic forces take power in Afghanistan. Pope Paul VI dies and is succeeded by John Paul I. Camp David summit concludes with a framework peace treaty ending 30 years of hostility between Israel and Egypt. Sudden death of Pope John Paul I who is succeeded by John Paul II.	Rice/Lloyd Webber, *Evita*. Blondie, *Parallel Lines*. Graham Greene, *The Human Factor*. John Irving, *The World According to Garp*. Harold Pinter, *Betrayal*. David Hard, *Plenty*. Films: *The Deer Hunter. Midnight Express. Superman*. TV: *Dallas. Grange Hill*.
USA and China open diplomatic relations. Vietnamese troops and Cambodian rebels capture Phnom Penh and oust the Khmer Rouge regime. Shah of Iran flees the country with his family. Egypt and Israel sign peace treaty in Washington DC. Iran is declared an Islamic Republic by Ayatollah Khomeini.	The Clash, *London Calling*. Boomtown Rats, *I don't like Mondays*. Italo Calvino, *If on a winter's night a traveller*. Peter Schaffer, *Amadeus*. Martin Sherman, *Bent*. Films: *Alien. Mad Max. Manhattan*. TV: *Antiques Roadshow. Life on Earth. Tinker, Tailor, Soldier, Spy*.

FURTHER READING

Kenneth O Morgan's biography, *Callaghan, A Life* (Oxford University Press, Oxford: 1997), has not only a vast amount of detail but also is rich in detail of the context in which Callaghan was making decisions. The late Prime Minister's autobiography *Time and Chance* (Collins, London: 1987) is also extremely useful but does not contain the same factual content.

Most useful are the diaries of two Cabinet contemporaries of Jim Callaghan, Harold Wilson's *The Labour Government 1964–70* (Penguin Books, Middlesex: 1974) and Richard Crossman *Diaries* (Condensed Version) edited by Anthony Howard (Methuen, London: 1979) both provide a detailed insight into Cabinet decisions Callaghan was involved in, and in the case of the Crossman Diaries contain personal comments on Callaghan's performance.

However, the above reading material gives a distinctly Westminster view of events, particularly so in the case of Callaghan's involvement with Northern Ireland. This is why I sought an Irish perspective which I found in Tim Pat Coogan's *The Troubles* (Robert Reinhart Publishers, Boulder, Colorado: 1997). This provides information regarding Northern Ireland which is rarely found in British sources. The same was also true when looking at wage restraint and the 'Winter of Discontent' when events are described from the standpoint of London-based commentators.

The reality is that in the British Isles there are a multiple of perspectives one of them being the Scottish perspective which was provided in *Guilty by Suspicion, a life & Labour*

(Argyll Publishing: 1997) which I wrote with Jimmy Allison the former Scottish Organiser of the Labour Party.

Roy Hattersley's *Fifty Years On* (Little, Brown, London: 1997) gives a wide view of the political scene when Callaghan held the great offices of state before becoming Prime Minister. It is also an easy read.

The diaries of Tony Benn covering the 'End of an Era' 1980–90 express personal opinions of Callaghan from Benn's political viewpoint which are both colourful and controversial and help towards providing a rounded viewpoint of Jim Callagan's political life.

Other books I have quoted from are Frank Chapple, *Sparks Fly, a Trade Union Life* (Michael Joseph Ltd, London: 1985), Angela Tuckett, *The Scottish Trades Union Congress: The First 80 Years 1897–1977* and David Kynaston, *The Financial Times A Centenary History* (Viking Adult, London: 1988), which provided little gems but in the main concentrated on other issues. Henry Kissinger's *Years of Renewal* (Simon & Schuster, New York: 2000) also falls into this category but throws a fascinating light on how Britain and the US approached the crisis in Cyprus in different ways, and also the high regard Kissinger had for Callaghan.

PICTURE SOURCES

Page 87
A photograph of James Callaghan as a Cabinet member in
November 1967. (Topham Picturepoint)

Pages 132–3
James Callaghan, as Foreign Secretary, photographed during
a visit to Uganda in July 1975. Standing next to him are
the Ugandan President Idi Amin and his special adviser
Dennis Hills. Callaghan would have to intercede a few
months later to prevent the execution of Hills by Amin.
(Topham Picturepoint)

INDEX

Welensky, Roy 31
White, Eirene 61
Wigg, Michael 19
Williams, Shirley 136
Willis, Norman 110
Wilson, Brian 125
Wilson, Harold 8, 18, 20,
24, 26, 34, 36, 37, 38,
39, 42, 43, 44, 45, 47,
48, 49, 50, 51, 52, 56,
59, 60, 61, 62, 63, 69,
70, 71, 76, 77, 81, 83,
84, 85, 89, 91, 92, 93,
140, 141, 143, 144, 146,
148
Witteveen, Johannes 98

Y
Young, Alf 129
Young, Arthur 70

THE 20 BRITISH PRIME MINISTERS
OF THE 20TH CENTURY

Boxed Set
(all 20 books plus
TIMELINE OF THE
20TH CENTURY
extra and only available
as part of the boxed set):
ISBN 1-904950-53-1